A FOOL'S JOURNEY

Veronica Y. M.

Copyright © 2023 More Wunder Publishing

All rights reserved

No part of this book may be reproduced, or stored in a retrieval system, or transmitted in any form or by any means, electronic, mechanical, photocopying, recording, or otherwise, without express written permission of the publisher.

ISBN: 979-8-9881704-1-9

morewunderp@yahoo.com

Illustration by: K. J. V. H.

TABLE OF CONTENTS

PART 1: SEARCHING FOR THE UNKNOWN   1

PART 2: UNEXPECTED GUIDANCE   29

PART 3: REAWAKENING   72

DEDICATION

For my amazing children, never stop learning all you can, especially about yourself. Thank you for coming to help me, being who you are, and reminding me to let the little things go. You are my inspiration, light, and everything, and I love you for eternity.

For my Buttercup, thank you for being with me during one of my loneliness and darkest moments. And all my family for your patience and help in our time of need. I am forever grateful and love you all unconditionally.

PREFACE

This is to be read with an open mind, no judgment, animosity, or resentment; just unconditional love for all. This is my story, written only from my perspective.

INTRODUCTION

Seventeen years have passed since my journey began. I have since learned; how to overcome fear, seek help, come to peace with my past, heal, let go, discover myself, root out negativity, love myself, and what unconditional love really means. I listened to my heart – my soul. I held onto faith. I believed, I trusted a higher power; I found my purpose; I found the greatest love – I had awakened. I want to share my story, hoping my light will help others find theirs.

PART 1

SEARCHING FOR THE UNKNOWN

Sitting here looking over God's beautiful creation. I never imagined how it would look from above—so many mountains, hills, and open space, primarily covered in powdery, white, sparkling snow. The shadows and lighting are incredible!! It's beautiful!! I'm so thankful for experiencing all of this. I've flown twice in my life before. I only remember the last time well. Every bump that shook the plane kept me alert; I could not relax. As my sister, mom, and I pulled up to the drive near the terminal entrance today, I told myself that I wasn't afraid or nervous and won't be, I'll be alright. And I was. I felt drained but okay. Since I had feared heights, I had hoped for a window seat. I must have been heard because I got that seat and could see the wing. I was ready to free myself from everything. I was prepared to listen. This was the beginning of my new life.

February 25, 2006

I have thought about my life, so far—many challenging times and heartbreaks. I wonder if, without those experiences, I would be who I have become. I felt I had accomplished a lot in the past five years. I was so close to dropping out of high school; if I had quit, I would then need to get a full-time job. I felt I would be trapped, and school was an endless knowledge of freedom. So, even though I mostly had D's and C's, I graduated. With an interest in computers, I enrolled in a local trade school. In the beginning, I had a tough time & was unsure if I would make it. But with the first ever real effort and determination, I graduated. This was the first time I knew I could accomplish anything I set my mind to. I started at a community college the same week as my graduation ceremony. With no real idea of what career I wanted, I felt the need to keep learning something. I felt lost when I wasn't in a classroom. As I continued going to school and working for four more years, I took a variety of classes, including ethics, which increased my questions in life. Since the age of 14, I had always wondered about everything in this world, Heaven, and God. I have been fascinated with astrology, always reading the weekly scopes, and at the end of the week, seeing how accurate it was to mine. It wasn't until 2001 that I began questioning it all. I started to study astrology and tarot. I believe there was something more powerful in them. I had put a lot of positive energy and time into learning these cards. I practice, practice, and practice on myself, family, then friends. I wasn't great, but fairly good and was getting better. I was always amazed at how much information would come through. I realized if I could understand others in the way they think, act, and feel. I can reflect on my own actions and how I think and feel. I can learn who I am. Around this time, I began watching this psychic woman; she regularly appeared on an afternoon talk show. This woman caught my attention; I would focus on everything she said. I began buying her books and would always make sure not to miss her appearance on the show. I knew she didn't have all the answers, but she was helping me see life differently and helped open my mind up to the possibilities of something greater. I believe we all are here for a reason and have a purpose. I didn't have a clue what mine was; I just felt there was something more to discover. I started diving deep into books and my life. I realized my life wasn't going anywhere; there was no real meaning. I felt I couldn't do much if I didn't know what I wanted.

As time passed, I got involved in a short-term relationship, triggering a range of emotions. My mind was nonstop day and night. I could no longer deny my heart's yearning for something more in life. I not only thought about myself but the world as it was & trying to understand how it came to be. "Why were so many people unhappy? Why weren't they finding and living for happiness? Why is there so much suffering? How did we allow the basics for life to be taken? How did people become so selfish, cruel, and heartless? How have so many souls forgotten why we are here?" All we seem to think about is money and how much we need for survival. Since I began paying bills, I have tried to stretch my dollar. I was lucky at times when I had a little extra. I was always broke. "Why should we live like this? That's no life. Why should a dollar determine who eats and stays warm? Why are we not searching for more?" I was sleeping less and less, missing work, and skipping classes. I could no longer ignore the feeling of something missing inside. I felt a strong deep feeling inside that I was supposed to do something greater. I didn't even know what it was or what direction to go, but I knew the way my life was falling apart wasn't good. I couldn't focus on how to get my life back on track. I was exhausted. My family was worried, I couldn't and didn't want to try to explain to my mother what I was going through. I couldn't make her understand; I didn't completely understand myself. I felt I was being judged and looked down on, that I was screwing up. I thought, at times, maybe I was mentally unstable. After the worst argument with my mother and sister, I packed and left. Drove around for hours looking for a decent, affordable hotel. I was at my lowest; I had never felt so alone. I knew going back to my old life was no option. I could no longer be where I was unhappy. I cried and prayed, prayed, and prayed for help and guidance. After falling asleep for a while, I was ready to listen to myself. By the second day, I had decided to stay with family in Southern California to clear my head. I booked a flight out of Colorado

Springs for a few days out, enough time to take personal time off work and talk to my mother and sister. I knew my decision would hurt others. It was the hardest thing I ever had to do. We had gone through so much together. We had grown close until I made a rapid change and pushed everyone away. The one person I was most afraid of telling, the one I knew would be so heartbroken, the one I couldn't bear to see cry–my one and only friend, my best friend–my sister. I was so nervous I kept practicing how I was going to tell her. When she got home from work, I held my emotions and told her. Her response was something like, "Oh well, whatever," in a calm disappointing tone, but her facial expression said something else. I could see the heartbreak in her eyes; she looked at our mother, turned around, and walked away. Mom went after her; I just couldn't. I could hear her cry. I couldn't bear to see her like that–especially because I caused that pain. She being 3 ½ years younger than me, I always felt I was her protector. I would try to shield her from nearly daily drunk yelling between our mother and stepfather. Many times, we would witness physical fights and objects being broken. I had to learn to block it all and try to stay in our bedroom, as did our older brother, but she wouldn't. Terrified, she would try to stand between them to stop the yelling and anger. I couldn't bear to hear her cry; I couldn't ignore her pain. I would always try to convince her to just come with me. I would do my best to ease her pain and comfort her. I felt so guilty knowing she now also had life questions, and I would not be there to help her. But I couldn't help her if I couldn't help myself. I knew she would be okay; I knew she was strong. I plan to be gone for two months, the longest and farthest we would be apart. I knew I was no longer getting anywhere. I was trying to keep pushing what had no longer served me. My mind was at battle with my heart. I kept asking myself if I was making the right decision. "Is this the right thing to do? Is this what I need? Would I find answers?" My mind would keep looping around to why I decided this in the first place. I was stressed, frustrated, depressed, confused, and lost. "I'm leaving because I need to focus 100% on myself and nothing else. I love my family more than anything; I know that much. I don't want to be away from them, I will miss them, but I've got to do this for me because only I can truly know what I want." I was anxious for change, and for what I hoped to discover. After many attempts to explain myself to my family, the day before I left, they finally were okay. Even through her pain, my sister saw my reasons. She, more than anyone, gave me the strength and courage to push through. If I didn't have her acceptance, it would have been an even more difficult journey.

The morning I left, it felt odd–surreal. It was clear and perfect. I was still in shock that I was doing this. I was always the predictable, responsible, and cautious one. We said our goodbyes, and off I was to start my journey. I knew everything would be forever different when I got on that plane. I knew I would be alright; it was the best thing for me. When I arrived, I realized how big the world really was. I felt so small, just another body, yet feeling I was here to accomplish something big, even if it was just for myself. I felt like I had entered a new world; as I watched everybody and everything, I thought, "Now what? What do I do now? What's next?" Again, I had to listen and reassure myself that everything would be okay; in time, answers would come. I started taking everything in. There were so many people! This place is so big that there seems to be no end! Life is constantly on the move, so ALIVE! "Were these people living for their ultimate happiness or just living?" I spent the 1st few days catching up on some needed rest.

Then I tagged along anywhere I could with my family. Being around them didn't feel as it had once before. Maybe because I changed, I see things differently. But it was wonderful to get to know them again. We had been close

when I was young. When I was 8, my mother married, and we moved to Colorado. For the first few years, we visited each other during summer. Financially it became difficult for everyone, so we saw each other less and less. As we grew older, we all became busier and busier, and we kept even less contact. Now, I had the opportunity to see who they had become, how they lived their lives, and get their perspective on life. They all worked hard. Even with a long work week, they made time for fun with family and friends. "Was that what I was missing? Do I need more people in my life to feel complete?" I had asked, "Which do they believe is best to listen to, your mind or heart?" Each response came to the same answer for different reasons. Your heart.
"Your heart is love and is where happiness lies. Your mind has no compassion but can reason. But both can play tricks on you."
"You can be blinded by love, and your mind can make you believe anything, even when it's unrealistic."
I went hiking with my cousin for the first time in the California mountains. She showed me that being your true self is the key to happiness, and without our true colors, we wouldn't have a beautiful rainbow.
I had spent time on my Tias' ranch. I saw the real beauty in life, the beauty in each soul we are blessed to meet and

share our love with. As my Tia said, "God knows what he is doing; put your trust in his hands." I knew this was all meant to be. I knew one day, this whole experience would be important and understood. I spent a lot of time reflecting and journaling everything, as well as continuing my tarot readings.

It was at this time I realized how ill my grandmother was. Complications from her diabetes cause her so much pain. I joined her on checkups, and as she talked with her doctor, I could see the agony in her eyes. Despite her pain, she turned to me, smiled, and waved. I could feel my face turn red and tears forming; my heart was broken. She was only getting worse; she had been suffering for a long time. About two years ago, we almost lost her. I remember praying and asking for more time with her. Now here I was, I had that chance. I gathered my strength and pushed my emotions deep inside. I continued to pray for her to heal, even though I knew in my heart her time was coming. I had learned she was the same sweet, warm, kind, loving, caring, and giving person I remember as a young child. As weeks passed, I began to worry about money as my savings were almost out. I needed to go back to work. I knew a decision must be made; my time to return home was quickly approaching. My mind was getting caught up in that circle again, questioning my next move. I was worried about how it would make others feel. Afraid I would screw up and be looked at as a failure. I felt I hadn't accomplished all I was set out to do. I was worried I would miss that key piece of the puzzle if I did nothing. But I knew I had to break away from any patterns that did no good for me, including trying harder to change my thinking. So even with mixed emotions, I felt I was ready for a change. I thought this was the place I should be. This is where I needed to be to find more answers. I would find that job I'm meant to do. I can get an apartment and start my new life out here. I felt torn between my family in Colorado and California. I felt with either choice; I would lose. I was afraid I would hurt someone. I was afraid my sister and I would never be close again. I felt she would think I abandoned her, and she may never understand me completely. I knew some who are a part of my life would be affected by my decisions, but I can't live my life through someone else's eyes. I have to experience & learn for myself; it's my journey. I had to find what my soul was yearning for. The one thing I did learn was that I was in love with life! I was excited to find that next piece and couldn't wait to feel its completion.

I was thrilled to be back home! It felt different, I felt different. I was happier. Everything and everyone seemed more peaceful and content. I was determined not to get off track and stay focused on my path. I went back to work right away and gave my notice. Within the next couple of months, I spent more time with my family. The thought of staying and making changes there came to mind, but the possibility of returning to the way it was, was terrifying. I would rather die than live as I was. The closer that time came, the more unsure I felt. I would cry and pray for a clear answer. My mind clouded my intuition. "Why would I change my mind?" I had no reason to. "Was it just cause I was afraid to feel the feelings of separation again? -Or because I think it's the wrong move?" I didn't want to think anymore, so I kept going, hoping it would be the right decision and leaving wouldn't be so difficult. I saved what I thought would be plenty to get started. My cousin flew out to drive back with me. I packed my truck with everything I could, including my cat, "Buttercup," and said our goodbyes. It was tough leaving. I didn't know when I would return home, but I had to keep going, even with tears and a broken heart. My cousin's upbeat personality and good music help ease the pain. She helped me get excited and hopeful for the future. Our road trip kept an energetic beat till about 8 hours later. My eyes couldn't handle just a few hours of driving, so she did most of it. With the more frequent rest stops, it took us much longer. I don't think she made it back on time for work; I felt horrible. I vowed to myself I would find a way to pay her back. The greatest gift of this trip was getting to know her even more; I was so grateful in a time of need; she was by my side. I was excited to start my new life. I envisioned the results would be similar to others, as I thought I was a late bloomer to life. The plan was to stay with family for a short while. I thought, with my education, getting a well-paying job would take no time. I figured in a couple of weeks, everything would fall in place and come together. I was sure that the next piece was that much closer.

A month and ½ later, I was still unemployed, and my savings were running low. With monthly bills I had to keep up with, I began to worry again. I started applying to anything, wondering how to make it on minimum wage. I ended up finding myself more alone and again questioning my decisions. With patience as my greatest challenge, it felt like time stood still. I thought I had waited long enough for happiness and fulfillment. "Why am I not moving forward? Did I miss something? What am I doing wrong? Did I make the right decision?" I kept positive and reminded myself that everything has its timing.

I finally got a job through a temp agency, but it would be a very short assignment, and I would soon be waiting for the call to the next job. I had also been in contact with a friend from back home, whom I knew had moved back to Southern California, and was over an hour away. We kept in touch by phone almost daily and did meet up a few times, which was nice also having a friend close by. My life was starting to move forward very slowly.

Then, while visiting my grandparents, suddenly, my grandmother got really sick and passed three days later. At a time when family should come together and celebrate her life, my family grew cold toward one another. I couldn't understand it. Even with the guilt of not doing things differently the days before she died, I understood her time here was done. Her love, kindness, and warmth will forever echo in my heart. I wished I could help heal my family's grieving hearts; it would have helped mine. I tried to help bring the family together, I then ended up getting caught up in the middle. I saw and felt what must have been in their hearts for a long time-deep anger and hurt. I was heartbroken, confused, and angry that my family could be like that. I found myself more alone, grieving the loss of all. I spend the next month mostly in solitude. I cried, cried, and prayed for healing for them all.

Sometime later, I was placed in another temporary position, which lasted several months. It was a relief that I would have something steadily coming in for a while. Then October 12, my journey came to another challenge. The landlord found out I had been staying longer than allowed at my Tias home, so I had to leave. I knew my uncle would have taken me in, I was sure his girlfriend would give him the message, and he would call me back immediately. I packed up my truck with everything I had, including "Butta." I told my Tia he said I could; I didn't want her to worry and didn't want to stay any minute longer in fear she may get reprimanded. As the day turned into night, I still hadn't heard anything. So, my SUV had to do it for the night. I wasn't sure what would be safest, to park in a high-traffic area or secluded. After driving around for hours looking for a perfect spot, I figured near the emergency entrance of a hospital would be just right. Even so, I barely slept, woke up to every little noise, and sometimes just to check my surroundings. The next day I wasn't sure what to do; I had to look at my options. I couldn't stay with others for similar reasons, no shelter would accept animals, and none of my family could take her in. I could either give in and go home or sleep in my truck. I didn't feel it was time to give up; I felt I had to stay on this path, even in the current circumstances. Even though I did feel ashamed and embarrassed, I didn't feel like a complete failure, as I know others would have viewed me. So, I didn't want anyone to know. So, I lied. When I would be asked whom I was staying with, I told them a friend from work and my mother with family she didn't speak to. Near my job was a small shopping center with a 24hr gym. Since I was a member, I would work out twice a day to use the showers. My truck was full of boxes and other stuff, every night I would move things around so Buttercup and I could rest better. It took a few nights before I felt safe and comfortable enough to sleep a few hours straight. I felt guilty for Butta. I hadn't realized until that moment what she had probably been feeling. I should have left her at home; I thought things would be different. I took her away from the only home she had known, where she was safe, warm, and happy; I told her how much I loved her and only wanted her to be with me. I tried to keep her comfortable and happy. On the other side of the gym was a small open field where I would let her out every morning. I did fear not knowing how long we would have to live like this. But I knew this time would pass, and there was a reason for everything. Soon, it became a routine. I would get up around 5 am, let her out, work out, shower and head to work. After work, I returned to our parking area, called for her, fed her, returned to the gym, and read and wrote. I would reflect on my day, the people I had been interacting with, and what I was to learn from them.

One night, I had awoken to a light shining through the back window of my truck. It was a security guard for the shopping center. He asked me why I was sleeping in my car and wasn't allowed in this lot. I told him that no shelter would take me and my cat, but I could go somewhere else if it was a problem. He said no, it's okay, just to be safe, and he will keep an eye on me on the nights he works; he left me his work number if I ever needed help. I could sense his empathy and his compassion. I don't remember his name, but I will never forget him as the Angel sent to watch over me. I was able to sleep much better afterward.

On days off, I would go to the library to use the internet for job searching. One day before leaving, I overheard a lady giving a speech for a career day event. She was talking about the challenges she had to go through to get to where she was. She had to work hard to get what she wanted, and that school was the way out. I listened to how well she made her speech and asked her afterward how she knew her passion. She said after a while, you would know, it would be your calling. She asked if I went to church, that it had helped her, and gave me the name and location of hers. I thought I might find answers there. So, the following Sunday, I showed up. Everyone was smiling, friendly, and happy. Even with everyone welcoming me, I felt I did not belong. When the

Pastor began service, the room lit up with lively energy! Once the room was packed, an offering bowl began being passed around. I watch others put something in. I had nothing to put in; I felt horrible. I had only hoped no one saw me pass it off. Then the Pastor continues saying, "Give to the house of God!" With how I felt, I thought, "What if they can't? Do they feel obligated? What if they never could put anything in? Would they still be welcome?" As the service continued, I was confused with what was being said. Seeing all these people unite for peace, harmony, love, and praise of a higher power was beautiful. But as soon as judgment and money come into play, it goes against what I believe. I didn't want to be present for something that I disagreed with. I felt God loves all unconditionally, and we are here to learn and love, period. As soon as the service was over, I left. But this experience wouldn't stop me from going to other churches in the future.

As weeks passed, it got bitterly colder. No matter how many layers of clothes I wore and a couple of heavy blankets, I could not get warm enough. I made sure that Butta was extra cozy and comfy, tucked in right next to me, under the blankets. I was frustrated and angry with myself at times. "Why can't I figure out whatever I am supposed to!? What am I not seeing!?" I began losing faith and questioning God.

I felt my prayers weren't being heard. Negative thoughts about self and everything filled my mind again. Even though I had been working, I struggled to keep up with my phone, truck, gym, and gas. I was stretching every dollar I had. I would buy whatever food I could with whatever was left. I felt weak; I found myself going to sleep most nights hungry. Then I caught a cold, which was getting worse. I was miserable; I didn't want to live like this anymore! I cried out of frustration, anger, and loneliness! I hadn't seen any family in weeks. I wanted to see my grandfather so badly, but I knew I would be asked where I was staying, and I didn't want to lie anymore. I thought a lot about my past, feeling all the pain from my childhood. Remembering when my stepfather was alive, the day I found out he died, and the day of his funeral. I thought about my grandmother, how I got to know her again, the week before she died, the moment she died, and the days after. I thought about home, our Sundays were the best. We were all home together one day of the week, just watching movies and relaxing. I was missing home so much. Why am I still here? What am I doing? I have experienced and learned so much, but this path may be exhausted. I had a dream that night, short and simple. My whole family was getting inside an elevator with others. A group of seniors and I didn't have time to get in when the elevator began falling.

The cable was about to break, I grabbed it and saved them. "Am I supposed to help save others? Am I afraid to lose the ones I love and care about? Do I have more control than I think? Or am I just missing the whole point?" All I was sure of was that I wasn't happy, but I thought I needed to give it more time.

A month later, my family back home found out the truth. I was told, "Just come home; it's not working out; what are you trying to prove?! Are you afraid to admit you made a mistake?! We knew $1000 wasn't enough!"...and I ran away from my problems, I was selfish, and I left my mother to care for our disabled brother instead of helping her. I apologize for making my mother worry; she would always worry. I couldn't quit just because they weren't happy with my decision. I felt they never had faith in me and had hoped I would fail, which hurt deeply. I will not live my life through someone else's eyes, no matter how much I love them! But to ease some of my mother's worries, I agreed that if nothing improved by the end of the month, I would go home. I definitely didn't want to go home *now*; this only pushed me more. I was determined more than ever to focus and take in everything; I would not leave with nothing.

One evening, a week before Thanksgiving, I called for Buttercup, but she didn't come. It was so cold out. I kept getting up to check for her. I cried; she always came to me. By morning I knew she probably wasn't coming back; something must have happened to her. I was heartbroken. "Where was my baby? Was she lost and scared? Was she calling and looking for me?" I searched for days. I wrote a description with contact information and distributed it to the surrounding businesses and neighboring houses on the other side of the field. I checked shelters, but nothing. I cried and cried and prayed to God, "Please bring her back to me! Tell her I'm so sorry! I love her! I promise we will go back home! Just come back to me!" But she was gone. I was crushed. I failed her. After a few more days, I knew there was no chance I would find her. So, I prayed and asked God, "Please, if she is still alive, keep her safe, warm, happy, and with plenty to eat. Tell her again I'm sorry that I tried to find her and love her with all my heart." I felt a piece of me was gone. My heart ached for a long time; I couldn't understand why she was taken out of my life just like that. I was filled with anger and regret; I should never have left home; everything was fine until I decided to search for who knows what. I couldn't forgive myself for not caring for her as she deserved. I tried to stay positive, but nothing good came out. My mind continued on a negative downward spiral. After Thanksgiving, the roller coaster continued. I was offered a side job designing an advertisement for a start-up business. It seemed hopeful, and I got to work on it right away. I started spending more overnights with that friend from back home, making that long 1 - 1 ½ hour drive; as well as more overnights with family, celebrating my 25th birthday and the holidays with them. I was tired of being alone. Just before Christmas, the security guard from the shopping center came across a woman who had said she found a cat from that location in the description of Buttercup. He was able to get her number for me. I was thrilled to hear she was safe! I was grateful she had her! I wanted her back badly, but I knew I couldn't care for her as she deserved. I asked the lady if she would continue to take care of her until I could, and she was happy to do so. I was so relieved I cried, prayed, and thanked God for watching over my Buttercup. Mid-January, my temporary job ended, and finding another was difficult. I know we need money to live in this world, but why do they make survival nearly impossible!? As for the other job, I was never paid after completing the work. Then my truck began giving me problems I couldn't afford to fix. I was tired of trying to figure out the next step. This deep yearning for something greater was still in me; I couldn't find a job to fulfill me. "What was this yearning for?" I'm searching for something unknown. "What if that something was nothing?" My fear was never knowing. The same old thoughts kept circling in my mind. By this point, my intuition was clouded. I felt, I'm continuing this journey blindly. The same questions, confusions, and emotions are all the same from back home. Yet, I still kept pushing forward.

A couple of months later, I began sleeping more nights in my truck and spending more time alone again. Thankfully, the nights were warmer. I was able to get a permanent part-time retail job and get the minimum done to keep my truck running. I no longer knew where to put my energy. The light seemed to keep moving further away. I was tired of my journey. I was exhausted. But something in me just wouldn't let go. I prayed and prayed for guidance. "If I could just see it, I would know where to focus my energy." I snatched up every opportunity of overtime I could. I would make sure my phone and gym were always paid. My truck was so far behind payments it was impossible to catch up. With whatever money I had left, I would put most towards gas and the rest on food, which meant cutting my intake even more. I tried a cup of noodles for a couple of weeks. But with no place to heat water every night, it wasn't working. I didn't want to fill up on junk, so I settled for anything healthier and lasting longer. So, one can of tuna and a medium bowl of diced watermelon a day was it. I would eat half for lunch and half for dinner every day. I actually never got tired of it. In the beginning, I was miserable; I was always hungry and felt weak. After a couple of weeks, my stomach shrank, and it became more bearable. I dropped even more weight, especially since it was getting hotter, which was great, but I would have rather done it an easier way, that's for sure. Luckily, once a month, I had an extra 2-4 dollars and could buy something extra to eat. When I wasn't working, I would watch the sunset every evening. Sometimes make the long drive to watch it set at the beach. It was the best part of the day. It's so beautiful, calm, and peaceful. I felt free; I felt closer to everything. My worries were let go, and my soul was filled with hope and inspiration.

I spent a lot of time reflecting, thinking, and writing. I thought back to two years ago, four years, then childhood. I had always known who God was by what I was taught growing up—God was loving and to be taken seriously. But I have always felt there was something greater and more loving. Even as a young child, it didn't make sense to see how the world portrayed God to be and how they used God to create fear. It felt wrong. I also didn't understand why our creator would allow us to hurt. "Why was the world such a horrible place? Why was there so much hate and anger? What's our purpose? Why was I here?" I didn't want to be here. I couldn't make sense of my world; I felt I didn't belong. I could feel there was a better place; I just didn't know where that was. I then thought more about the hurtful parts of my life. As soon as the hurt and anger came rushing back, it was enough to stop and move on. I hated to think about the past; it's over and done with, no need to carry it into my future. I learned more this year, especially this last month than in my whole life. "Even knowing what I now know, where will it take me? How can my life experience get me anywhere in *this* world?" Then it hit me; this journey was only about me, nothing more. To really know who I am! It's not for a job to define me, not validation from someone else. It was for me to find my power in my truth from what I feel so strong inside. To stand strong with determination, to not be persuaded by anyone. I found a piece of my puzzle; I know there is a lot more I have yet to discover. But I had been heading in the right direction! This is what I had to do to figure it out! I was already doing what needed to be done! It makes sense now. I have learned that I have yet to come across a single soul that meets my connection. I have overwhelming deep compassion for everyone, that I just can't be unsympathetic. Something is calling me and telling me to share my story, help save this world, help spread positive energy, help open up others' minds, and lead them to their light. Yet, I'm still trying to figure out what to share; it's not much. I feel closer to that yearning, but not as close as I had hoped I would be this far along. I kept having dreams of my past, memories I had forgotten. Some, where my future was looking into my past. "Am I supposed to share my past? Is the key in my past? But what exactly?" By the time it was March, I had found myself spending two or three weekends a month with that friend, and I began falling deeply for him. When May arrived, it was time to head home for my sister's college graduation. My mother and sister purchased me a round-trip airline ticket. It was wonderful to be home! There have been a lot of changes! They had moved, my brother was receiving treatment, and now my sister was graduating! They all seemed happy and doing well. I was incredibly proud of my sister. She worked hard and hung in there. I felt I was being looked at in disappointment and being reminded that if I hadn't left school, I would have been graduating along my sister's side. But I was. I no longer cared what others thought of me. I knew what I had accomplished and what it took to get where I was. The week seemed to fly by, and it was already time to return. This time, I didn't want to leave. That's when I knew this path was getting close to an end. If, in six months, I can't get a decent-paying job and a place to live, it would be time to come home.

Weeks after returning to California, I found myself spending more time alone. That "friend" began making excuses not to get together. But then randomly called after 10 pm to make time for us. I just quit trying and caring.

In the months that followed, nothing had changed. I was still being let down. I was tired of feeling unworthy and used. I was still unhappy. I was tired of being alone. It was time to close this chapter. I said my goodbyes to everyone and thanked my family for what they had done and given me. Each of their encouragement, advice, and love was more pieces of my puzzle.

"Whatever challenges come our way, just be strong, keep your faith, and everything will be alright. It's just part of our path."

"Life is easier when you are open to communication and to speak from your heart."

"The life you live is the life you created. If you want better, you must push yourself to succeed."

"Your life is more meaningful and enjoyable when you share it with others."

"Always carry a smile and love in your heart."

With a one-way ticket on 08/26/2007, I made the long uncomfortable journey home on the greyhound. I reflected on what I had learned, who I met and tried to understand why we crossed paths. There was a wonderful loving feeling in each of the many souls I had the opportunity to meet. There was something in knowing someone else's story. I was fascinated to hear where they've come from. I heard so much joy and felt the love when they spoke of their loved ones. I felt their pain as they spoke of their losses. I understood their struggles to survive. I saw many working so hard, some pushing themselves dangerously to the limit to give their families as much as possible. Others were so tired all they wanted to do was get through the day. They all seemed lost, lost in this illusion. They felt powerless and trapped. I wished I could help ease their pain and struggles, but I couldn't. All I could give was a piece of myself; my advice, love, compassion, understanding heart, hope, and inspiration. In return, they all gave me the edges of my jigsaw. I felt there was a greater meaning to this whole experience. I still couldn't understand it yet. I had changed, inside and out (45 lbs lighter). I discovered who I am, what I can overcome, and how strong I really am, and I'm free to live my life my way.

PART 2

UNEXPECTED GUIDANCE

Being home took a while to adjust to. There were mixed feelings about me returning because of my leaving in the first place. After an emotional start, everything began going smoothly. I stopped thinking about what the next piece would be. I didn't give up; I was just tired; I wanted to take things as they came, at least for a while. I took the first full time job offered, and now that I could eat more regularly, I watched my diet and made sure to make it to the gym 4-5 days a week. All those little annoying things family does didn't bother me; I missed everything about them. I spent as much time with my family as I could. Slowly our relationship began rebuilding. Being home for the holidays was odd, a new place, new friends, just a new feeling. I also decided not to take Buttercup back; it wouldn't be right to take her away from her current home. The lady was more than happy to continue to care for her; she even sent me a photo of Buttercup, safe and happy. As for my heart, I was still deeply in love and missing that friend. We kept in contact almost daily. As time passed, I kept busy with family and friends; I spent less and less time on the phone. Which helped make it easier to let him go more. Then he asks to spend New Year's Eve together. I hesitated but said yes. I decided to have one last weekend with him, then say goodbye forever and move on. I flew to San Diego on 12/28 and returned home on the first. I was disappointed it didn't turn out as I'd hoped, but he kept me hanging on a little longer. I reverted to the daily communications, and he made a trip out to see me in April. Even though I was happy to see him, I was tired of how it was. Something had to change, and I was not moving back. My mind was made up.

After some time, he made a decision also. In July 2008, he and his kids moved back to Colorado, where I had a place set up for us all. I was so excited and nervous to finally see my new life unfold! We had all got along well. Having my little family and more people to share my life with was a great feeling. The first few weekends, we either spent time at family gatherings or just relaxing together at home. We never had extra money; being a Sagittarius, I couldn't just sit in all day, so I would think of simple outdoor activities to do together, which the kids enjoyed and was a terrific way to bond with them. By the second month, nothing was what I had imagined, more came to light what we didn't have in common. When I would come home from work, we barely carried on a conversation; all he wanted to do was watch tv & did not want to be interrupted. I would spend most evenings alone, so I would read and write. I began questioning myself if I had made a mistake. "Was I desperate to be loved that I kept trying to fill a void and pushing this relationship? But shouldn't it be enough that he is here with me? Why can't I just be satisfied?!" That emptiness began returning. Maybe I need to change things up and just keep myself busy. I started spending more time at the gym during the week, most times out on weekends, and stopped thinking he was waiting for me to come home. After some more time, that feeling continued to grow. I knew I needed to figure it out. I had never wanted children of my own before. I thought this was a horrible world to bring a child into. But I see things differently now, "Maybe that's the emptiness missing in me. What would it feel like to carry and nurture a child from day one? What would I teach my child? How can I protect them? Can I guide them in the right direction? What would I do differently?" A child of my own may give my life more meaning and solid direction. I always believed there was a reason for everything. So, I prayed and gave it to God.

At the end of October 2008, I found out I would be bringing another soul into this world! I was excited and terrified at the same time! "Can I really guide her in the right direction? Can I really do everything to protect her? Can I prepare her for THIS world?" She will be looking to me for answers, for guidance. There's a reason she chose me. I thought back to what must have been her conception. I had felt what must have been her soul entering my body! It was the most amazing, beautiful feeling! I knew I had to show her a better world. Not only to understand and respect all life and that LOVE is all that matters, but I felt there was more – something else I had yet to answer.

I thought with a new one coming into the picture, her father and I would become closer, and things would change. But it was more of an eye-opener of *finding* my worth. Early into my first trimester, I had a bit of bleeding. I was terrified something was wrong. When I asked to be driven to the hospital, he hesitated and said no, because it would be really late by the time he got home to make dinner. I was so shocked; I couldn't believe him! From this moment, how I saw him change. I called my sister, and she and her friend drove me. Everything turned out fine; it was completely normal this early on. When I got home, he apologized and said he should have just taken me. I was so hurt and angry, I just stayed alone in the bedroom. For the first few weeks, I got really hungry here and there. I wanted to do everything right for my baby. I would eat a reasonable amount of what I could find that was healthy. He told me I shouldn't be eating so much, that I would hate myself in nine months. That hurt. Yet, I said nothing. I was judged my whole life on my appearance, so his remark really hit me hard. I held in my emotions and tried to stay out of sight. I felt ashamed, disgusting, embarrassed, and unloved. I hated being home. I questioned my future with him. But now I'm carrying his child. "What should I do? Am I overthinking everything? Am I being too sensitive?" I tried not to eat, only if I got really hungry. So, I spent more time with my mother and sister and ate with them before going home. I tried to keep a positive mindset and do my best to be all healthy for my baby. She and I were now my only focus. We continued going to the gym, enjoyed walks, relaxed to music, read, write, and spent more time smiling and laughing. This was the most incredible experience! I never felt so connected to another soul!!

On June 16, 2009, our beautiful, healthy baby girl entered this world. The deepest, most beautiful love I ever felt. There was something about her. Something different. Maybe because this was a new kind of love felt. Or how she opened her eyes and would look at everything like she was taking it all in and trying to figure out where she was. Nothing meant more to me. I was afraid of the world around my baby. I wanted to put her back in me; I felt I could protect her better. I spent many nights waking up throughout the night to make sure she was breathing. I would spend many hours just watching her, wondering where she was before she came to me. "Why me?" I would try to imagine what she would look like all grown up. "What would her life be like? How would this world be to her? What is her purpose?" I was terrified something was going to happen to her. I was afraid to lose her. I began having horrible thoughts of something happening to her and even imagining hurting her myself. I was able to ignore and push those thoughts aside, and some days really fought to push them out. I didn't know these were signs of postpartum. She was never in any danger. Whenever these thoughts came across, I put her in a safe place within her father's or my view. I didn't talk to anyone; I figured there was no need if I recognized them and put them out. I wish I had, living in that type of fear was a horrible feeling. As weeks passed, those thoughts came less and less until they were gone. When I had to return to work, I hated it. I felt I was always away. When I got home, it was close to 5 pm; she was in bed by 7. I had 2 hours a day with her. That hurt deeply. All I wanted to do was be with her. I wanted to see all her firsts. Some evenings I would fall asleep early, just laying in bed next to her crib to spend more time near her. As months passed, it began to be our routine. Just me and her an hour before her bedtime. I would read to her, then rock her in my arms as I sang her to sleep. This was the only routine I always looked forward to, just her and I peacefully side by side.

By Christmas, we were shocked to discover we would be expecting again. This time I was careful, but I was ecstatic for my daughter to have a sibling close in age. Yet questioning why another baby with him. By the time I was in my second trimester, I was exhausted. I couldn't afford to take time off, plus I hadn't accumulated any more FMLA. After a while, I started missing work. Which eventually caused me to lose my job. Fortunately, I was able to collect unemployment. But it wasn't enough to stay where we were, so we found a smaller place around the corner from my mother and sister. His daughter had already been moved out to further her education at a distance. With his son, I wanted him to live with us. But he moved in with his grandfather so that he wouldn't change schools. This was when I learned I had no say regarding his kids and would be quickly dismissed. In the back of my mind, I would question our relationship. It wasn't horrible, but it was not what I thought it would be. At times I would feel used, unloved, and just there. But I just kept hoping things would get better between us and just tried to keep my focus on my baby girl and preparing for the new little one coming.

This pregnancy was the opposite of the first, probably because my body didn't heal fully. I had no energy, didn't exercise, but was able to eat healthier; as I got closer to my due date, I felt heavier. I was ready for this kid to come out! Two weeks after moving, on July 24, 2010, we welcomed our beautiful, healthy baby boy. As I held that little guy close, he pulled me deeply in. Such a happy baby, nothing but smiles. I know God sent these two beautiful souls to give me more meaning and a sense of direction, and I will try my all to guide them on the right path.

There was a peaceful, comforting feeling with a new home and a new baby. But it wouldn't last long, as we continued to argue, I knew deep down that my feelings for him were changing, and soon it would become easier to let go. I didn't want that to happen; I was afraid I might never know what could have been.

Two months later, I found out that some household finances had stopped coming in – a month before we had moved. Which now meant we could not afford the rent. My mother and sister took us in with no other place to go. I was grateful I had a family to help us but embarrassed. With two parents, we shouldn't be in this situation at all. But he did find a job almost immediately. I continued to look for work when I had free time, which wasn't often. I was so busy juggling housework, appointments, and two babies most days and nights alone. My anxiety, feeling overwhelmed, and depression had returned and was increasing. After Thanksgiving, it all became too much. After a kind gesture from the baby's dad trying to help me organize, all I saw was a mess. I lost it; I became hysterical, yelling and crying. I grabbed the keys and took off. I spent the next 3 hrs alone. I knew this wasn't normal or healthy. It was time to talk to my doctor as well as my family. Everyone was great and supportive. It was quick and simple. One daily pill made me feel calm, happy, and less anxious. I quickly learned not to miss a dose, as I became dependent on them. I felt free of my emotions. All those horrible feelings were pushed far down inside and hopefully be gone forever. I was more relaxed, which made it easier to juggle less. I was a much more pleasant person to be around, that's for sure. My relationship with everyone was more peaceful, and it continued to be enjoyable over the next 14 months. When I could, I took time for the gym, hiking, and had an entire Saturday to climb Pikes Peak. My love relationship seemed like we would get close to the top of the hill, then fall back down. I was hesitant to continue, as we had far more uncommon. But I still didn't want to give up and figured once we had our own place again, it would put less of a strain on us. Plus, things will improve now that *I* am on medication. I just tried to stay positive and focus on what we do have. Finally, in November 2011, we moved into our place. He would work mid-day shifts for weeks, then switch to evenings or overnights. I was still looking for work. I never liked the idea of daycare, having a stranger watch my babies, so it wouldn't be an option. I would keep looking for something to fit when I had time. Quickly after moving in, I instantly regretted it; I had less help and still doing everything, day and night. He would sleep all day until it was time to go to work and an entire day on his day off. As weeks passed, we barely carried on a conversation. He would hardly interact with our babies or any of the kids. I had no doubt he loved them, but it was obvious we were not on the same page on raising children.

As often as we addressed the same issues repeatedly, I could no longer deny the truth. I wanted more from life. I was no longer happy, and it became clear. I became more stressed, we argued more, and I did a lot of yelling. I saw how our babies were terrified and crying, I didn't want them to be around anger and fear. I didn't want them to experience what I had as a child. It was time to make a change. It wasn't easy telling him I would be leaving and taking babies with me. I don't think he believed I would. I soon found a part-time job as a merchandiser, leaving babies with him during the day, his evening schedule now consistent. I was working 20-25 hours a week, which I loved. The pay was excellent; with no one watching over my shoulder, I felt free, peacefully traveling within and just outside the city. With more time alone, I had more time to think. I thought of how free I would feel from those low emotions between him and I. I was ready for a change! Unsure how I would do this alone, I talked to my mother, and without hesitation, she was willing to help me. In March 2012, with my tax refund, we began moving into a three bedroom, three-bath rental house. My babies would finally have their own shared room, so much space to run around and play! I was excited for change and a peaceful new way of being. But deep down, I was hurting for leaving a part of my life behind. When the last bit of stuff was loaded, and it was time to gather the babies and say goodbye, that moment was the hardest. He put his face into his hands and wouldn't look up or say anything. I knew he was crying; something I'd never seen him do. My heart ached for his; I didn't want to hurt him. I wanted to go over and hold him and tell him never mind; I would stay. But I didn't; I couldn't; as much as my heart will always love him, it was time for me to go. Our time together is over. This chapter was done.

I carried that pain I had caused him for a long time. As I moved on, I tried to understand why things turned out as they did and what if I had given us more time. I would replay all I did try. I even remember telling him my feelings for him were changing. He would do things differently for a week or two, then return to his ways. I was so deeply in love with him that I feared losing that. And little by little, I did. That fear turned to anger, which I also carried for a long while. He continued to watch babies 3-4 days a week, most times at his place. Seeing him felt awkward; many fresh emotions were still there. At the end of the first week, I began noticing at pickup; they were not being cared for as they should. I knew it would be an adjustment for him, and he wouldn't do things as I would; I didn't want to be picky, so I just let it be. But towards end of the next week, they were clearly being neglected, because he was still sleeping all day, they were being left unattended, still coming home extremely hungry, and a couple of times, their 14-year-old brother would look after them (I think two toddlers all day is too much at this age).

So now there was no option but to put them in daycare. I couldn't afford it, so I applied for assistance. I searched for the cleanest and safest centers, which had secured entrances, cameras, half walls between classrooms, and plenty of staff. It felt safe, eyes everywhere. Even so, I still had a talk with my babies about letting me know if someone isn't nice to them. They cried every morning, my son longer. Even after a few weeks, my son still struggled to adjust. I figured it was normal. When I would walk my daughter to her class first, sometimes her teacher would tell my son he would be in their class for a few hours or the day. His emotions would instantly change, and he became so happy. I didn't put any more thought into it. I was so consumed with work, finances, and tasks at home. I always tried to finish my route early to pick them up before their afternoon nap. Sometimes I would get there just after they had lied down, and my son usually was crying. Then one afternoon, my son told me that the teacher was mean and hit him on his bottom. At 2, he usually would say things to get what he wanted; I sat with what was said for a moment but figured maybe it was because he just wanted me to be with him, I didn't listen or pay attention to the signs of distress. I would regret it, years later he could clearly tell me about the mistreatment he and many other children around his age and younger had to endure from a childcare worker. Also, how other teachers were aware and would comfort the children, but nothing was done to protect them.

As time passed, their father would come to see them twice a week, then once every two weeks, to once a month. They would always ask for him, we would call him, but he usually wouldn't answer. I couldn't understand why he would do them like that, to go so many days without seeing them, to hurt them like this. When he would call back, I would calmly explain how they were feeling and that he needed to see them regularly. He assured them he would on his days off, which he did, just a couple of times–then reverted to being away for another period. I was constantly calling him, pushing him to make time for them. So eventually, he was willing to watch them once a week, instead of having them go to daycare. I chose the shortest shift of the week. That way, he would stay alert, care for them the right way, make it as easy as possible for *HIM*, and usually take them to his place. They were thrilled; at least they got some comfort in seeing him once a week.

Even though I was earning what a full-time job paid, it still was tight. Their dad would help with a little bit of money but nothing regularly. I was trying to be considerate with how I left him in a place he could barely pay for himself. So, I didn't want to keep asking for money. I just needed to manage my money better. As months passed, their father was helping me less and less. Then, I found out he had a live-in girlfriend; it hurt how quickly I was replaced and made me think if I *was* being used. "How is it he didn't have time for his kids but plenty for a woman? So now he has help with rent, so why wasn't he helping me more?" I was so angry I demanded he needed to help more regularly every month. I told him I would file for child support if he didn't, and in turn, he threatened to take them away. It took a couple of months to get a child support order in effect. With some untruths he told, he was only required to pay $258 total a month!! I spend about $55 a month on just diapers and pull-ups!! I was so angry; it's just not enough for two growing toddlers! For the next four months, even though it wasn't always peaceful living with my mother, everything was going well for the most part. Then all of a sudden, my hours were slowly decreasing. I didn't know my hours were based on sales, and being winter, energy drinks sold less.

After the cold months, it would start picking up again. With what I made during that time; I didn't want to just quit. This would become a new problem at home. I was now falling short on my half of the bills. I felt guilty, my mother works very hard, and their father and I should provide 100% for our babies. Had I known this would happen, I would've waited to move in with her and looked for something else. She was constantly pushing me to quit and take any 9-5 job. I just couldn't; that would mean my babies would be in childcare all day. Someone else would be raising them. I would hardly see them. It didn't feel right. They came to me for a reason; I could feel it deep down. I needed to be their teacher; I needed to guide them. She couldn't understand; she and many others see life in one direction. I knew I still needed to provide for them, but I refused to do it her or anyone else's way. I just needed to try harder to find a second job. I tried my best to juggle two toddlers, work, looking for additional work, and cleaning. But it wasn't good enough. My mother would constantly be on me about toys being left around, dishes not being done, just always something. It wasn't dirty or cluttered; it just wasn't constantly tidy. When I wasn't job hunting, I felt I needed to be doing housework, or she would get upset; I would do what I could to please her. The continued stress was now affecting my sleep. I became more frustrated and low on patience and began yelling at my babies if they wouldn't pick up their toys. I would discipline my kids as I would *think* my mother would want me to. Even to the point of spanking my son once and my daughter twice. Something clicked that second time with my daughter; she didn't cry; she just stared at me, and I stared at her. I walked out, questioning what I had done. My heart broke, and I cried so deeply. I love them; why would I hurt them?

What have I done? I went back into the room; she had tears; I grabbed and hugged her so tight and cried and told her I was so very sorry; I love her so much and will never do that again. And I never had. At that moment, I realized something wasn't right about how my mother's influence was over me. I became the parent I always frowned on. It was hard to have time to put more thought into everything, so I prayed. "God, please help me be a better, more patient, and loving mother to my children. Please forgive me; let them forgive me. Please keep them safe from everyone, even me. Please help guide me." I wasn't going to let anything, or anyone, get in the way of being better to them and raising them as I had always intended. I put their love, happiness, and joy first. I would put play and nap time before any house chores. Nap time was one of the best times together. Not only was I getting the much-needed rest, but to just lay there holding them and not thinking about anything else, just peacefully being together; nothing else mattered.

By August 2013, I found a second merchandising job, 5-10 hours a week. With great pay and the product was a wide range of snacks that had great sales throughout the year, with a few hours I could count on. So, with both jobs, I could always have a steady income. Thankfully, it worked out perfectly. The kid's father would come to watch them for those few hours. He was alert and active with them, so they had more quality time. I finally had that balance I wanted, to spend time and provide for them.

By October, everything was more peaceful between their father and me. When I got home, they were well cared for and happy. He began coming by for a bit, even on some days off. We started talking more, his girlfriend moved out, and he had been doing things differently; he'd changed his ways and wanted us to try working things out again. I had seen a difference; a part of me missed him; I missed the deep conversations we would have, when we had them; it was a wonderful feeling having him around. I wanted to stay hopeful, but deep down, I felt doubt. But I ignored it. I told him, let's see how it goes with a little more time.

In November 2013, sales plummeted even more with my first job, so they needed to cut back on merchandisers, and positions would end in mid-January. Because of my time with them, I was offered a full-time job as a sales rep, which would require 50-60 hours a week and great pay. At the same time, my second job also offered me a sales position, which would be about 30 hrs a week, earning more, but less than the other offer. I was okay with that; I would rather be home with my babies. So, I turned down the first offer and accepted the second. My supervisor told me he would get with me before that job starts the second week of December. I put in my notice for the end of November for the first job, so I can be 100% ready for my new position. I thought, wow, finally, everything is falling into place! It all seemed clear!! Then December came, and the start date kept being pushed back. Then suddenly my hours were becoming less and less, costing more gas than I was making. I was frustrated but trying to stay patient. The kid's father kept consistent; everything between him & I was going great. So, I decided to give us another try, and he would sign the lease & move in a few months. My mother was happy for us and began looking for another place.

Just after January, my supervisor said they could not open another sales rep position. I was so angry I quit. And it was way too late for the other job offer. I now had to start looking for other employment. But I figured it would be easy, and now that the baby's father will be in the same home again, things will be different and go smoother. When March arrived, it was time to renew our lease. I was still out of work; he said with 100% certainty he would move in. With his new job and his income alone, we could still sign the lease. My mom found a duplex to rent just down the street from us. I spent the first few days very busy, helping move my mother in, which included all the living and dining room furniture. I cleaned up our house and began planning where all our old furniture he had would go. I was expecting him to show up with everything, but strangely, I had yet to hear from him. I would call him, and he said he still had to wrap things up. He began just stopping by for a bit before work, which I wanted to put less thought into; I figured he was still getting things done between work. It was just babies and I spending all our time together, which I absolutely loved.

Days turned into weeks, and he would come less and less. Each time I called him, he wouldn't answer my question about what was going on, which I couldn't make sense of because he was paying rent. I had assumed his other lease had ended or at least about to. Since I wasn't working and with his recent job change, child support stopped, I was completely broke. When it was absolutely necessary, I would call to ask him for money for pull-ups and other basic needs. He would always ask for what and wasn't pleased about it, but he would come to bring the amount needed. His demeanor was different; he seemed stressed and upset. We would see him again when I needed more, which wouldn't be for 3-4 weeks. My feelings were telling me something was not right. My heart broke for my babies when they would cry asking for him; I would say he was working or still packing. I couldn't understand what he was doing, I didn't know what to think. I felt like a fool. "Was this to get back at me for leaving him? Had I made things worse for my babies?" I tried to keep them busy so they wouldn't think about him. We would play together more and have fun with all the empty space in that big house. I was worried though; this didn't seem like him. I kept telling myself he would show up with a truck full of his belongings and happy to start over.

I just needed to find a job to help, and we will be okay. By June, I had tried to keep my mind and emotions calm. I would tell myself, "He's still paying rent; why would he do that and not move in, so the only thing that makes sense is that his lease must not be up yet. I'm sure it must be at the end of this month. It wouldn't make sense if it weren't soon." He's probably just really busy getting things in order. I just need to be patient."

At the end of the month, our family unexpectedly welcomed my beautiful niece at four months prematurely. Understandable fear filled everyone; there were constant prayers from all friends and family near and far. I felt she would be okay, but I needed to know for sure. So as fear loomed in my mind, I pushed it out and listened for the truth to flow. I was overcome with calmness and comfort and knew instantly this was confirmation she would be fine. She came here as she did for a reason, to give hope that miracles are possible. Today, she is an adorable, strong, smart, and healthy little girl. Over the next few weeks, I tried not to put much thought into the home situation and focused more on going to the hospital to see my sister and niece. What was most important was right in front of me, *life* is most precious and nothing else truly matters. Yet when our sense of security is threatened, we suddenly fall into complete despair and are blinded to what God is trying to make clear. Toward the end of July, a notice was left on the front door; rent was past due, so I called him. That's when he told me he couldn't pay for our rent and his apartment; it was too much. I was so confused! I asked, "Why are you paying for an apartment when you were supposed to live with us?!" He still wouldn't tell me anything. I had no clue when his lease would end. I was so upset; it didn't make sense. "What was he not telling me!? What am I supposed to do!? I'm not working, I have two toddlers here!?" But just like that, he wouldn't answer my calls. My mind was nonstop, I screwed up. "Why did I think things would be better!? Why didn't I just move on!? There was no way I could come up with the rent, plus now late fees! And now also fallen behind on my truck payments!! I'm stuck. I'm such a fool, I'm an idiot! What's wrong with me!?" I ignored the landlord's calls for several days and just sat around in disbelief, not making a plan.

I would hide my emotions from my babies, once they were in bed, I would just cry and cry. I was so angry with myself, I just wanted to give up, there was no way out of this. "I'm a horrible mother!! How could I let this happen!? What am I going to do!?" I felt so ashamed and embarrassed. "I will have to tell my babies, daddy will not be living with us, and we will have to move. I will have to break their hearts." I talked to my mother; she offered to let us stay with her. As the fees began adding up each day that passed, I finally called the landlord back and explained the situation. I slowly started packing and looking for an affordable storage unit. It was a matter of time before we would be officially kicked out. Then the utilities were turned off, which he also quit paying. After a couple of days, with no utilities, we stayed nights at my mother's place. I would head back during the day to continue packing. With the whole legal process, it was official, I now had about 15 days to vacate. It was now rush time, I didn't have time to sell what didn't fit in storage, so a lot was donated or thrown out. I wanted to avoid as many charges as possible, so with my mom's help, we cleaned up really well. Then it was time to say goodbye to our home. That was really hard, especially for my babies. I just kept telling them something better would come; it would be okay. A part of me knew that was the truth.

My heart ached for losing the home they loved so much. I let my babies down. I failed. "Why…why did I let this happen?? How am I going to get out of this hole?" I was now at my heaviest; I felt so disgusted with myself, such an idiot, a fool, an embarrassment. I didn't want to try anymore. I just wanted to cry and sleep, but I couldn't even do that. I needed to be strong for my babies. So now here we were, in my mother's duplex, the kids and I sleeping in her spare bedroom. Extremely grateful for her help, guilty for invading her space. Knowing how my mother is very particular with her home, I once again felt like I was walking on eggshells and trying to keep my babies toys in just the room, constantly cleaning and picking up. I was stressed all the time. I was able to find a job, another merchandising position. Yet it only lasted a very short while. What I was earning basically just covered the cost of gas.

Then one day, I received a letter from an attorney's office representing the rental property with a bill of just under $4000. It included not just the portion of breaking the lease, but a list of charges for repairs and cleaning, which I knew was a load of crap. But I didn't want to fight it; I didn't have the energy, and besides, I screwed up. The utilities also sent what was owed, which I had no idea how much was unpaid, which came close to $2000. I know I will be stuck with all of it; I was not counting on his help after how he did us.

Three months later, I found a full-time job at a call center. As much as I didn't want to have my babies in a daycare center all day, I didn't have an option. Their father was no longer helping, not even coming to see them, just making phone calls inconsistently.

When my tax refund came, I went to the attorney's office to pay off what I owed. That was a lot of money, but I was relieved it wouldn't any longer be hanging over my head. Now, I need to save a bit more and get us an apartment with no issues. After a couple more months of saving, I had enough to get started in a new place. Lol...yeah...well, was I in for a surprise. All that money I paid was basically for nothing. I could not find any place that would accept an eviction; it didn't matter that the debt was paid off! I was so angry! How unfair and wrong!! "Yes, I did screw up!! It was my fault!! I know this, but I did my part and paid what was asked for!! So why do I need to be punished!! Things happen; people aren't perfect!! What am I going to do now!? How am I ever going to get us a home??!!" Had I known, I wouldn't have paid off that debt. "I'm such an idiot, I just can't make the right decisions!!"

I thought I learned all there was about credit. When I was 18, I got my first pre-approved credit card. Making minimum wage, I was doing fine, making payments month after month. Then more cards came, which I kept opening. Before I knew it, I had around 10, anywhere from $200 to $500 each. As soon as I was late with one payment, it went downhill. The late fees were so high, and to add up with what was already due, I just kept falling more behind; it was impossible to catch up. By the time I was 23, I had filed for bankruptcy. Since then, I have tried to keep clear of any credit cards or owing anything more than a car payment & student loans. I have always hated money. The way it's valued is horrible. It's not balanced fairly. "How is our survival all based on money? How much you have determines if you'll be warm, clothed, and fed. Why? Why do we have to fight for basic needs? I just don't understand this world." I was so hurt and angry with myself, with God.
"Why wasn't God helping me!!?? Why was it always something?! What have I done!!?? I don't deserve these babies, I can't do anything right, I keep failing them!!" Negative thoughts would be automatic, almost continuously in my mind. Now my weight has begun affecting me. It was taking my energy and interrupting my sleep. I was depressed, even though I hadn't missed any pills. I had

extreme insomnia and anxiety that I started missing work, which caused me to get written up, then a final warning. After a few weeks, it got so bad that I eventually had an anxiety attack, missed work, and lost my job. My doctor sent me to do a sleep study; I was diagnosed with sleep apnea, which my weight was a major factor. Even though I hated having that machine to sleep with, I was so grateful I was able to sleep.

Now back to square one, it was time to focus on the job hunt. I was again applying anywhere possible. Even with child support back on track for a while, it still wasn't enough, and once again, falling behind with my truck & phone payments.

After some time, a minimum wage, part-time retail department store called me. I wasn't thrilled, but very grateful. I started working mostly evenings and weekends and again starting a new routine. My mother would care for my babies. But after a few months, I again found myself getting fewer hours. "How can I afford anything on 5-10 hours a week!? It's just not enough." I couldn't seem to be able to stay ahead. I didn't know what to do anymore. I hated being in this world. Anything I do fails. "Why is this all happening? What's the point of all this?! Are we all here to struggle and suffer?! I hate it!! I just hate it!!" I didn't want to waste more time there, so I didn't return and decided to go through an agency. Luckily, it was perfect timing for seasonal positions, which would last for a couple of months and would be more hours per week. Then a couple of weeks after this assignment ended, a temp to a possible permanent position was offered, because of my education. I was thrilled; finally, my schooling was paying off!! It's about time!! Full-time, really great pay, and in a clean room environment!! I was so happy and determined to put my all into this job. It was challenging at first, as anything new can be. But my trainer was great; she constantly told me how well I was doing. I was so relieved and happy. I finally felt I was heading in the right direction. My world seemed lighter, smoother, and my prayers were being answered. Finally, everything is falling into place! I had no worries; I was confident I would be brought on. I plan on how much I can offer to double or triple the amount for a deposit to get into an apartment. Then, one morning as I was getting ready to head to work, I got a call not to return, that I was not a fit. I was disappointed, but shocked once I was told why. My trainer had been telling her supervisor I wasn't doing well the whole time!! That I had not made any progress! I was so upset and in disbelief!! "What, why, how?! She had been lying to me!! And lying about me!! Smiling and acting kind towards me!! I knew I felt something off about her!!" I went straight to talk to her supervisor, I explained how she had been telling me I was doing great, but it didn't change anything. It didn't make sense. I finally was where I was comfortable. It really crushed me. I couldn't understand why this was all happening. I really wanted this. I needed this! I got into my truck, drove, and parked where no one could see me. I cried and cried so deeply. I was extremely frustrated; I didn't know what to do anymore or where to put my energy. I felt worthless, useless. I'm never going to get anywhere. Nothing makes any sense. I didn't want any family to know how much this tore me down, but I think they knew how much I really wanted this. After a couple of weeks, the agency got me into another temp to a possibly permanent job. By this point, I didn't care. I was angry with God; I felt unheard, worthless, forgotten, and unimportant. I didn't want to put any energy into any job anymore. I will do whatever job that comes my way, and if it doesn't work out, no biggie, move on to another, as long as I keep earning whatever money I can for my babies. This new position would be minimum wage making tools in the evenings and right next to my mother's work. So, I put my babies in the childcare center around the corner, I would drop them off, and my mother would pick them up within two hours when she got off. It worked out perfectly. It went smoothly, again. After a couple of months of a steady income, I was feeling better; I was able to start saving a little at a time. Old thoughts and questions about life would still cross my mind. I would try to push them out, I didn't want to waste my energy or time with them anymore. It's not doing me any good or getting me anywhere. If I had ignored them many years ago, I would have gone in a different direction and done things differently. Of course, I would never undo my babies, but I could have chosen a better path down to the right career and been able to give them so much more they deserve. I was then given "good" news that I would be placed permanently. I should have been happy and relieved, but I had mixed emotions and that deep nagging yearning pulling more. I envisioned being there for years and years. Living the same day over and over, and just being. "Yea, I would be able to provide for my babies, probably need a second job to make ends meet…and…if I did, I wouldn't ever be home with them, I wouldn't do anything more but live to work…I wouldn't be able to raise them as I intended, they would be raised by strangers and the way of this world. What would be the point of being here if I was just going to *be*?" The fear of living with this deep yearning in my soul unfulfilled felt like I was suffocating, dying slowly. My anxiety was ramp, and I hardly slept that night. The next day I continued my routine with uncertainty. After dropping my babies off at daycare, I headed to work and started my shift with hesitation. I was very anxious but pushed out all those emotions and told myself, "I need to keep working; I need money." When lunchtime came, I went up to the break room and just sat there, listening, and watching my coworkers happily carry on. "Why couldn't I just be content? Why can't I be like them, satisfied? Why can't I ignore these emotions, this deep yearning!!" I was screaming inside, I couldn't breathe! "I want out of this prison!!" I couldn't take it anymore; I got up and walked out. I felt an instant relief, fresh air, and freedom as I drove away. Yet, I wanted to cry. I knew I needed to work; I needed that job. I thought of turning around and going back, but the thought of that heavy energy stopped me from changing my mind. "Why can't I be like everyone else!? Why can't I ignore these feelings!? What will I tell my mother? I can't tell her I quit; she will be so upset. It's not right for her to do all she has been doing; I owe her so much." I decided to tell her the assignment had ended. I hated lying, but I really didn't want to hear anything more than what I already knew. Since I had walked off the job, this agency would no longer help me. So, I was back to square one. Either way, I needed to do more for my babies, and I wasn't, I struggled to find something to fit us. It became more of a struggle and stressful living with my mother. I understood where she was coming from, I couldn't get her to understand my perspective. I couldn't deal with her negativity, judgment, and criticism anymore. One night I could no longer take it, I packed my truck, and we left. We stayed about three weeks with a close friend, who is more like a father to me and grandfather to my babies. He welcomed us with open arms, no judgment, and lots of love and kindness. The energy was lighter, I was able to clear my mind and focus on what I wanted and needed to do. I took more time to pray peacefully and ask for guidance and help. I felt so refreshed and ready to push forward with determination. After talking again to my mother, we moved back with her. I really didn't want to, but she was the only one who would help watch my babies. She did back off a bit, though.

To add to the stress was dealing with the continued inconsistency of their father, still only calling randomly. It had been about four months since he had seen them. They would still cry, asking for him. Then one day, he happened to call wanting to see them. I had told him what he'd put them through, how much they'd missed him. He sat them down and promised he would come to see them more. They were happy, I was delighted and relieved for them, I just hoped he would keep his word.

As months passed, that wasn't the case. He went from coming to see them once a week, to once every two weeks, to once a month again, then three months would pass. My son was more expressive with his emotions, even saying he would hurt himself and sometimes would. My daughter was the opposite; I couldn't read her. On a couple of occasions, she broke down, crying so deeply, asking why daddy didn't love them. The worst pain was not being able to take their pain away. It was like watching them grieve for him. I was so angry with him. "Why does he do this!? He is so selfish!" I no longer knew how to help them; I didn't know what to say. I didn't want this to cause any lasting damage, I couldn't just do nothing. It was time for professional help, but not just for them, I needed it also. My goal was to resolve current issues so I could be better for my children and get some guidance to get back on track. Little did I know it would lead me to the past I thought was done with.

So, the three of us began our weekly session separately, talking to a stranger about why I was there felt awkward. I felt I was going to be judged. I explained what my kids were going through, he asked how I felt about it all, then he said something I had never considered. My children probably felt these emotions because they were picking up on mine. It made sense. I was stressed and had so many mixed feelings. My energy was affecting theirs. It was an awe moment. I needed to change this energy. I needed to be more aware of how I was feeling around them. I thought, "Okay, I'm good now." But nope, that was only the beginning. As weeks passed, the babies therapist didn't see anything abnormal, which I figured after what I learned from my sessions. It was decided their father was better off not in their lives, if he was not going to be consistent. I've never kept him from them, ever till now. I made more of an effort each day to pay attention to my thoughts and emotions around them. It truly made a significant difference. They were happier, my son stopped hurting and speaking horribly about himself. By this point, they stop asking for their daddy less and less. So now it was time to do some healing for myself. I thought, "What does my past have to do with anything?" I wasn't entirely comfortable talking about my deepest feelings I've never shared with another soul. It took several sessions to really open up. I had to go backward to my earliest memory and then forward through the painful memories, which I dreaded. I kept a lot of myself out and didn't address all my pain. When it came to talking about my mother, that was where most of the healing was needed.

Our relationship never felt close. When she married my stepfather, was when I felt more of a distance. My perspective of life really began changing. I didn't feel my stepfather cared much for me, especially my brother, his demeanor towards us felt different than our sister's. She was only 3, he adored her. I wasn't jealous, I just didn't understand why he disliked us. I wasn't a heavy kid, but not a thin one either. I was always called chunky by my family; it was a nickname all my life. But it never felt in a degrading manner, and it didn't bother me. But when he began teasing me, it felt different, maybe because he was new in my life or because it felt out of disgust. My mother knew it bothered me, yet she allowed it. Sometime later, we moved from California to Colorado, and that's when everything changed. Saying goodbye to our entire family was the first real pain I'd experienced. Leaving behind all I ever knew, where I felt so loved. I was hurting so deeply to go home. But instead of comfort, it was more teasing, belittling and jokes at my expense, and now also by my mother and siblings. This was when I began feeling really alone, confused, and unloved. We ended up moving to the middle of nowhere with just four neighbors. My mother and stepfather worked in town, about 45 mins away, with only one car, he had to be at work before the sun was up, so they had to ride together. We were left alone till after dark. We would get ourselves up and ready to catch the school bus. My brother, who was about 10, was to look after us. It didn't go so well. He had changed. Not only did he tease me, but he became very physically abusive toward me and sometimes our sister. There were days we all had fun and played together, memories I will always cherish. But most days were a nightmare. I was afraid to go home after school. My sister and I shared a room, so I would try to plan how to avoid him and go straight to our room. We would barricade ourselves until our parents got home. The furniture was too heavy to move, so we piled whatever we could lift against that door. We tried to tell our mother how he was treating us, but she would just say, "I don't want to hear it." Just having them home was a relief, knowing he couldn't hurt us. When summer came, it felt like it would never end. We would try to get up early before he was up to use the bathroom, grab food and barricade ourselves all day in that hot room. My sister and I would look out for each other, listening when he was in the shower to make another run for food and use the other bathroom. Most times, he would try to push the door open. We spent hours pushing with all our might against that door. Even through the pain in our cramping wrists, we were too afraid to let down our guard. Once, he grabbed a large kitchen knife and began swinging it violently underneath the door. All I could think of was to put all my strength against that door and tell my sister to grab everything she could to put against that door. I was so terrified, "what if he could open the door? Would he really stab us?!" I needed to keep my sister safe. We needed to put heavier stuff against that door, as soon as I could hear him far away, I would trade spots with her, and with all I could push some of the lighter heavy furniture until there was no chance he could get through. We knew we had to tell mom, but yet again, she didn't want to hear anything. As soon as she got home, she was busy. Straight away to make dinner, get us cleaned up, fed, then to bed. We lived like this for about two years. We watch our parents drink so much to the point of continuously yelling, arguing, punching holes in walls, and physical fights. I was always filled with fear, not knowing what would happen. One night I had awoken terrified, I felt like something was after just me. I ran to the bathroom, which was directly across from my bedroom, and with all I could, held the door shut. I cried. I thought about running across the living room to my mom, but unsure if I would get yelled at for waking them, so I convinced myself it was too dark. It felt like something was outside the door waiting for me. I've never felt that kind of fear. All I could think of was to pray to God, "Please help me, please help me." I'm unsure how long I was there, but it began getting light outside. Then all of a sudden, that fear was completely gone, I just wanted to go to bed, I didn't care what or if anything was outside that door. I kept that night to myself, and that fear never returned. From this moment, I began keeping more to myself and not asking for help from anyone, but God if I needed it.

The teasing was now happening at school, while the belittling at home escalated. One night as we sat for dinner, my stepfather was at it again, everyone laughing at his hurtful words about my weight. I tried to ignore it and push my emotions deep down; he came up behind me and yanked on my ponytail hard enough to make me fall backward in the chair to the floor. I cried and ran to my room. My mom came in a few minutes later, telling me he was only playing, and convinced me to finish dinner. I didn't feel any sympathy or compassion from her. I was so confused as to why she had changed so much toward me. "Why did she allow someone to treat me so poorly?" I really began questioning her love for me. I was only nine and really started hating myself, so much so that I tried ending my life. One night I got up when everyone was asleep, grabbed a wire hanger, and went into the bathroom. As I silently cried so deeply, I unwound the hanger, put it around my neck, and started twisting it tighter and tighter. I just wanted to leave this world, I didn't know where I would go, I just knew it was better than this place. I kept begging God, "Please take me, I don't want to be here! Please! Please!" I could feel the pressure in my neck and head as I twisted it tighter and tighter. Then, the fear of the pain of dying crossed my mind. So, I stopped twisting and just sat with my back against that door. After a few minutes, I was calm, I stopped crying and began hesitating. It was like my emotions had just turned off. I unwound the hanger and sat in that spot for a long while. I then got up and just went to bed. And just like that, the fear of my parents fighting, my brother, or anything out to hurt me was gone. Anger and hatred build up against myself more and more. Most of this time after, I blank out.

Moving forward, my therapist wanted me to either have my mother join in on one of my sessions or write a letter to her. I didn't want either, but I wanted to move pass this. I needed to heal and let go. So, I wrote a three-page letter. When it came time to read it to her, it was the most uncomfortable moment. I felt she wasn't really taking in what I was expressing, I felt she was judging me. I felt guilty for any feelings she may be feeling toward herself. I got an apology and a sense of guilt, but honestly, I didn't feel much empathy. I didn't feel as relieved as I had hoped. But it was done, I just wanted to move on. I thought I was good now, it was out, and I could wrap up my sessions. At the same time, because of certain circumstances, a family member revealed a secret from a much later time. It felt like a slap in the face. "I'm such a fool, an embarrassment for dragging my pettiness out." I felt I was being judged for complaining about something that was nothing to what they went through. "How can I think what I went through was comparable?" My heart broke, I always tried to protect them. I thought I was keeping them safe, but I didn't, I couldn't. It made sense why we grew apart. It wasn't me changing, but their trauma, a deep pain, a secret kept for years. What I had suspected, I wish I had done things differently. But I couldn't, all I could do was support and help them heal. I wanted all I brought up about myself to be forgotten and tried to avoid any talks my sister would bring up. I would continue to keep my emotions tucked away deep inside. But those emotions would overtake me once it was bedtime, and my babies were out. The same noise was running through my mind, over and over…"I'm such an idiot, worthless, disgusting, useless…I'm never going to get anywhere…I don't deserve these babies…I can't take care of them…I should have been braver when I was nine…I don't want to be here anymore. But I can't leave my babies behind. Who would love them as

I do? Who would teach them the most important things in life? Who would guide them in the right direction?" I honestly didn't know what to do. It didn't seem what I did would make any difference. "But what would happen if I did absolutely nothing?" I couldn't give up. I will take it one step at a time. I would job hunt throughout the day and wait for another agency to find me a position. I continued my daily routines with my babies, and when I had a little spare time, I would watch music videos online. That's when I came across conspiracy theorists. I began watching and listening to what they had to say. The thought of what was possible in the negative sense, it drew me in. I didn't believe it all, but a few caught my attention. I began researching what they made sound so convincing. I then began falling for it. I knew not everything is what it seems. Each time I followed these videos, I was increasingly pulled into them. It didn't fill me with fear, but the thought of how to prepare to live in a more chaotic unbalanced world. I would cautiously bring up my findings to my family, and they would play it off. This mindset stayed with me for months, even with nothing happening in the world.

One evening as I was scrolling for new information, I came across an older woman's video. The caption said something about a new world, so I clicked it expecting something similar to what I'd been listening to. But to my surprise, it was something completely different. She caught me off guard. She talked about what she discovered as a hypnotist, about beyond life and why we are here. Some confirmed what I had already felt, but so much more I had once wondered about. And *just* like that, she pulled me out of the darkness, she reignited my light with hers. I felt so much peace and strong positive energy. I couldn't stop thinking about what she said. I could never look at life the same again, my mind was wide open, and I needed to know more. I hadn't put this amount of deep thought into life as I once did years ago. This felt like a familiar pull toward all the unanswered questions I once had. I've always believed everything happens for a reason. "So why had I come across her video? Why now? Did I fall away from the light into the darkness of fear-based energies online? Was the need for that yearning to be answered that I stumbled in the wrong direction?" Whatever the reason, little did I know this would lead me to amazing discoveries about myself.

PART 3

REAWAKENING

Not much later, the employment agency found me another great job. Again, temp to possible permanent. Also, my education made me best suited for this job. A full-time, clean room environment with really great pay, the most I've ever earned. The only challenge was 12-hour shifts, 7pm7am, three / four days weekly rotation. The first few weeks were tough because I was still homeschooling kids right after work. I was exhausted but willing to do everything possible to make it work. I didn't want to lose this job, "I will not screw up," I was determined to save up and get a home for my kids.

At about the same time, marijuana just became legal. I was so curious I decided to give it a try, it went from amazing to too much. After some time and trying other methods, it became mind-opening! I was able to block out all the noise of the world and hear every thought inside! So much information flooded my mind! So much clarity to almost everything that had been blocking me! The darkness was pushed out even more. I just wanted to write and write, that is when I could. It wasn't until I was working that I was able to put deep thoughts into those old and new questions of life. I had more energy and felt more optimistic. It felt like all the toxins were flushed out of my mind. I would only use it a few times for a couple of months, then stop. I wanted to play it safe in case I was brought on permanently. After several months, I received great news that I would be brought on for good. I couldn't have been happier. By this time, I had fully adjusted to my schedule. Such a huge relief, "finally...finally, I will give my babies a home." Everything seemed to flow easily and peacefully. I found a lovely two-bedroom apartment with a balcony, exactly what I wanted. Getting approved was smooth, I just had to pay a double deposit. We moved in November 2016. With what I was making, I didn't think it would be as tight as it was, still working on catching up on my truck payments and carefully budgeting every penny, but it was okay, we had a home, and that's all that mattered.

Nothing made me happier than seeing my kids happy. After two years of sharing a one-bedroom, I wanted to give them their own space. So, each had their room fixed as they wanted, and I would sleep on the sofa bed in the living room. It was well organized and cozy, with a few boxes stacked in the corner until I could afford shelving. It was like a huge weight lifted, a feeling of some freedom, just having our own home.

For the next few months, little by little, I allowed the kid's father back into their lives as long as he continued to prove his consistency. By now, kids got use to not having him around, they wouldn't ask for him, and if something came up and he couldn't make it, it would no longer affect them. Life had a peaceful and smooth routine. As usual, some days were more challenging than others. With 3-4 days off every other week, it was terrific! We spent more quality time together at home. Most times, a couple of those days, kids spent more time playing in their room, alone and together. Which gave me more time to myself. I usually relax and watch tv, then begin listening to astrology, and tarot readings, then found more videos / talks of that one hypnotic lady. Which really got my mind going. Now and then, I would go out on the balcony, enjoy some marijuana (make sure kids didn't see me), sit and write a little.

In April, at work one evening in a meeting, a request was made for more employees to volunteer to be cross trained in other departments. I thought it would be great for me, the more I could learn, the more valuable an employee I would be and the more I could make. I can slowly move up. I will make this place my life career. I'm set. So, I spoke to my manager, and she was thrilled, even the supervisor came up and thanked me for my decision. I was immediately moved to a more demanding, quicker pace department. I figured this would definitely keep me more awake and alert by constantly moving. But that quickly changed. This required me to be on my feet for 11 out of a 12-hour shift (no wonder why no one wanted to work in this department). It was painful, I was nowhere near used to being on my feet for that length of time. I was extremely exhausted, but I needed to give it time, I tried my best to manage. I did all I could to stay off my feet when I got home, even on my days off. After two weeks, not only were my feet still not used to it, but my knees felt weak, even to the point where they almost gave in a few times, so now it was about safety. I'm sure I would have been fired if I dropped a cassette full of products worth more than a house. So, I talked to my manager and requested to return to my old department or move to another. But she refused, which didn't make sense since I was the one who volunteered. I reiterated why I couldn't be on my feet for that length of time, so I was sent home and could not return until I had a doctor's note. I was so upset it didn't make sense, but it should be quick to get that note and return to work. But my doctor didn't want to just write one, he would rather see me first. So, I would need to wait for his next available appointment, which was about a month and a half out.

Fortunately, I was able to collect short-term disability through work. With income coming in, plus my tax refund in savings, I was good with it and figured it would be a nice break. Then once I have that note, I can return to my old department or another bearable one and go back to my routine. I took the first few days skipping household chores, resting, relaxing, watching movies, and playing with kids. Then it was a new relaxed routine covering lessons more easily, knowing we had all day. By early evening after dinner, I had even more time to myself. I began getting high more out on the balcony. It was so peaceful; the energy felt so calm, a perfect view into the sky to see a couple of full moons. I would stay up late and fall into deep meditation. I would write more. So much just came flowing out of me! First, I thought of the love I felt for my children. How much they mean to me, and what I would do for them. Then I thought back through the years, how much they've grown from birth. To the question of where they were before they came to me. They are my heroes, I was lost, lonely, and confused before them. The day we met in this world was when I felt what real love was. I had them as they had me. They changed my life. They taught me patience and unconditional love. I'm more loving to all, including myself. They are helping guide me in guiding them. I dug out my old journals from 11 years, four months, and five days ago. Re-read them all. I thought about everything, what it taught me, and how much I've grown since then. After all these years, a part of me never forgot, but so many details I had put far back in my mind. Still, I need to keep learning, more experience brings more knowledge. This time the universe forced me down this path, we have a home, it's peaceful, and the timing couldn't be better. It's time to really look into my past, to figure out who I was and who I am now. So much of my past still holding me back filled me with hurt & anger. Which meant I hadn't yet healed from them as I had thought. So, remembering what I learned from my therapist, it was time to face it once in for all. I continued backward in time. From a year ago, two years, four, six, and further.

At 22, it was the first loss of a family member I'd experienced. My stepfather suddenly unexpectedly passed. My heart ached knowing he was no longer in this world with us, but I not only knew he was okay in a better place, I felt it. I didn't grieve as others did, I grieved for them. I couldn't take their pain away; I wished I had been able to get them to understand what I felt. I was judged for my "lack of grievance" in their eyes.

At 17, my sister and I were in a severe car accident; miraculously, she wasn't killed or severely injured. As usual, I would have given my sister the front passenger seat that evening, but something inside urged me to take that seat. As I'm always about safety, we all buckled up, yet her seat belt didn't lock in as it should have. When the car came to a spinning stop, and I turned to check on her (belt still buckled), she wasn't there and saw her about 40 feet away; I was frantically hysterical. I thought she was gone, but then she awoke. This instant rush of peace overcame me, and I just knew she would be fine. I couldn't understand why I was pushed to sit in the front and why this happened to her. But I knew she had Angels with her, she had a concussion, a few bruises, and sprains, but nothing broken.

At 15, we had moved several times, friends had become distant, and many new challenges were overcome. So, any questions I once had about life were pushed far back in my mind, almost forgotten. My brother was diagnosed with Schizophrenia, which became more severe as he got older. We knew nothing about this mental disorder, so in the years that followed, my mother, sister & I decided to take a 6-week class. Even with the understanding, it was nowhere completely understood and learned than the daily face-to face experience. He was extremely aggressive when he wasn't stable, which was quite often. I was always on edge, looking over my shoulder, needing to know where he was, and trying to keep my distance. I would rarely get a good night's sleep, not only afraid he would attack someone as they slept but trying to sleep with his music blasted throughout the night. I hated living like this, but my heart couldn't give up on him. Learning to adapt to his constant changes was probably nowhere as difficult as it must have been for him. At times he was terrified and confused, he looked so exhausted, there was nothing I / we could do. He is the most challenging patient most doctors and crisis facilities have dealt with. Some gave up on him and no longer wanted him as a patient, others would medicate him to sleep in their care for several days, then send him home, knowing he wasn't stable. The kind of desperate help he and many others need is there but isn't given, sometimes only available in extreme cases, such as after a crime. Unfortunately, this would be the case for him, and he was able to get the treatment he needed. It wasn't smooth and left us with many questions about the future. We were constantly involved in every facility he was in to ensure he was being cared for as he should.

By the time I was 13, my parents divorced, and we moved into a small two-bedroom trailer where almost every weekend was packed with my mother's friends partying past midnight. My brother was still at times abusive but was now able to have friends over, so he left my sister and me alone most days. From Friday after school until Sunday night, I could do and go wherever I wanted. For a 13-year-old, it was fantastic, and an entirely new way of living. I now had a couple of friends, but I never was truly myself. For a while, I was happy, it was a wonderful change. About a year later, the partying became too much, it was rarely quiet. Some weekends ended with so much drama, anger, fighting, and tension. The behavior of some of the men had become inappropriate toward underage young ladies. This was when my friend began changing, at times wasn't always the kindness toward me, but more so now around others. Some of these men would say hurtful things and make jokes at my expense. Yet I allowed it all. Since I was 7, I was always told how horrible I looked, I was disgusting because of my weight, ugly and dumb. As much as it hurt each time, by each person, I would rather accept it than be alone (even though I began feeling alone). Besides, I figured it must be true if more than one person saw this about me. I just need to be at the bottom, I don't deserve anything better. Yet when I saw others being treated poorly, my heart broke. I wanted to comfort them and tell them how beautiful and important they were. I wanted to heal them from any pain they had. My mind constantly thought about how I wished I could help others and make this world better. What also stood out at this time was when one day an ordinary conversation my friend and I were having with a friend of my mother's turned into something I had never forgotten and only just understood. She casually asked us, "Do you know what my favorite thing is?" In my mind, the thought of "Angels" came up. Nothing about what we were talking about would have given me that thought. But I ignored it, afraid I would be judged and laughed at, as usual. So, I said "Clothes." Her response was, "*Angels*." I was shocked, "How did I know? Why didn't I say that?" But instead, I kept silent and kept that to myself. I had always thought back to that, didn't know what to think about it. I would spend many nights gazing up at the stars, wondering what was beyond this place, "Where do I come from? Why am I here?" My curiosity and questions began growing, as well as confusion. From about 12 to eight, my world rapidly changed. I went from having so many people around, happy, and feeling loved *to* isolated, unhappy, and feeling unloved. I had very low self-esteem and felt ashamed of how I looked. I kept to myself, I was that kid who sat in the back of the class, hoping not to be noticed. I struggled in school; I couldn't understand why learning what was being taught was so important. I was always falling behind, then eventually placed in a "special" class, and diagnosed with Dyslexia. My mind was always wandering; I spent most of my time watching others, studying the world around me, and trying to make sense of this place. I had always felt different. I wasn't sure what made me different, but I felt it. I had a tough time expressing what I felt or thought. I couldn't form my words together to be understood. Which was one of the other things I was teased about for much of my life. I was kind to everyone but wasn't always treated the same in return. Yet I didn't change, even when I wanted to. I didn't understand the strong anger people would have towards one another. "Why do so many lack compassion?" I was always seeking acceptance, trying to find where I would fit in. I would quickly put my wants and needs last to please someone else.

Before the age of seven, I only remembered bits and pieces. I was a happy, carefree kid, loving and felt loved. I kept many of my thoughts to myself and still just trying to understand others. I remember as much as I could, many wonderful, cherished memories and more than I wanted that scarred me. Then I began writing everything from what I remembered that affected me to what I felt in those moments, as an adult, young adult, teenager, and even as a child. I cried. Then it was time to understand why some events happened and why I was treated as I was. Some were easier to let go of; others needed more healing & understanding. I closed my eyes and returned to those memories of that little girl, who felt so lost, confused, and unloved, and cried as I held her, brought that understanding to her, and let her feel how loved she was. *Instantly*, I felt lighter, happier, and more at peace. That energy I had once felt years ago returned. That deep yearning for more filled me. Something inside kept telling me to share what I have learned so far and to come. That my journey will help guide others to their light. I still had yet to understand mine fully though. I didn't just want to meditate and write, I needed to. So, I did every chance I got. This was when I began noticing what was happening as I was deep into my meditative writings. I was able to focus on a point in my mind where these thoughts outside of my own were coming through. I was having a conversation with someone else. It always spoke kindly, only the truth, encouraging me to push through and not give up. I couldn't believe what I discovered I was able to do. It was the same messages from many years ago, they had always communicated with me.

Message:

"Share your story."

"Will open their minds…spread positive energy…to help save the world…"

"Don't let fear hide your light…"

"Just let go…"

More than a month later, with the help of marijuana, I was able to balance my emotions, to meditate and focus on healing my past, and with ease to taper off my medication. As soon as I had that doctor's note, it was time to head back to work, and that free time became less and less. My doctor required me to have a mat to stand on, if possible since it's a clean room, which they couldn't do, as well as a five-minute break off my feet every hour. Unfortunately, I had to remain in that same department. Even with the disappointment of returning to work, I continued to do my best.

As weeks passed, the breaks did help from the pain in my knees, but my feet were still unbearable. I was exhausted all the time; I had no energy for myself. I had become more unhappy. I dreaded going to work, I felt like my soul was crushing, that I would be forever stuck in another meaningless job, an endless loop of nothing. Home no longer felt cozy, clean, and comfortable. Not only did we keep getting roaches in the kitchen, but now in the bathroom, hallways, and bedroom - just *everywhere*. No matter how many times pest control came, they wouldn't go away. "Why does it always have to be something? Why couldn't things just go smoothly!? Why had all this reawakened inside of me?" I just wanted - *needed* to write. That's what I felt pulled to do. I needed to stay connected. "How can I discover more answers about myself and my purpose if I don't have time?"

Once I arrived to start my shift, as well as on breaks, to help me zone out and bring my mind to focus on sorting through my thoughts as I mindlessly worked, I would take a hit of my marijuana vape pen. Which did help me get through several shifts, but after some time, it became where I didn't want to be there anymore. So, I decided during my lunch break to walk away with no plan whatsoever. I didn't put any thought into my action until a couple of weeks later. I then realized what I had in savings won't last but another month. Now my mind started racing with confusion, I didn't want us living here anymore, yet I had no job or money for another place. I started gathering everything I had that was worth something to pawn, which wasn't much. When the following month arrived, I couldn't come up with the entire rent. I didn't want to ask for help, as once again, I felt ashamed for putting us in this situation. As well as being reminded how selfish I was, among other things. The regret eventually came as I saw the sorrow in my kid's eyes again. I assured them we would get another home, a better one without roaches. I could have attended the court date for the eviction and just told them the apartment was infested and they couldn't clear it up. It's possible the judge would have sided with me, and my rental history won't show another eviction. I should have gone, but I needed time to move everything into another storage unit, as this time, I would need to do it all alone. I packed and moved everything from the second-level apartment to the rental truck to the storage unit, except for the sofa bed, which the kid's father did help with. As well as he would let us stay with him, his older daughter, and her boyfriend, in their two-bedroom apartment until I got us another place. I had to keep reminding myself that I wasn't leaving with nothing. The one thing that stood out more than anything was the reawakening. The familiar feeling of that deep yearning and the new discoveries filled me with hope, not fear.

Kids were happy to see their dad daily. It felt awkward for me, it took a while before feeling comfortable. I couldn't make him the kind of father I felt kids deserved. He was chosen for their lives for a reason, to give them something to take for their journeys, I needed to accept him as he was. This was also an opportunity to mend the past with him. I had thought about us and why he was meant to come into my life. The feelings I felt with him are what ignited my awakening when my journey began. This type of connection with him taught me so much about myself.

When the kids were at school, one day a week, I would go hiking for 2-3 hours. Being in nature was so rejuvenating to my soul. I felt free; a reset, I would reflect and write.

Journal: 08-12/2017

-Going backward again to the earliest memory, through each emotion and understanding...

-Remind myself, even more, to remember who I am and how far I've come...to be broken down again, to be brought back further up...I can master anything...I will always move forward...

-Just like hiking, not looking down as often, to balance...

-I wasn't leaving anything behind or failing, I was gaining more knowledge to shine brighter...

-I had always been on the path to finding greatness, we all are...

-I still feel down knowing I haven't gotten anywhere in this world...fear of nothing changing still fills me...

Meditative writing:

"If it's a struggle, let go, try it differently."

"Make adjustments."

-How can I succeed in this world by being me? Where do I belong? Why can't I just be like everyone else?...

-If I can get their acceptance, I can get their understanding, in hopes I can help them feel as I do...

-Excitement fills me to feel what I will discover, what I will share, and how I will help...to feel more connected. One morning, what started to be another day of job hunting turned out to be amazing. I attended a group job interview, which I didn't really want the job, but felt I needed to go. During a break, I knew it was a waste of time. As many people began walking out, a young lady needed a ride home. I happily offered. I felt something different yet familiar about her. As we began talking on the drive, it was like speaking to myself at 24! Everything she said was where my mind was at that age! I'd never met any other soul like this! I was in such disbelief to hear about her journey, challenges and where she was planning to go. As I dropped her off, I told her, "Just keep shining your light," which brought her to tears as she shared with me an experience she had hearing those exact words many years before. It just clicked for me. I wasn't meant to go to that interview for that job, it was to cross paths with her. So, she and I would see we were not alone, we needed each other at that moment to help encourage each other not to give up. I've always been terrible with names, but her name never left me, and every time I question why I'm as I am or feel alone, I remember her.

Not too much longer after this encounter, I had the apartment to myself. I decided to take advantage of the time to meditate. Didn't expect anything different from any other time. I pushed out all worries, mind noises, and little surrounding sounds. Open my mind from within and let whatever flow through without judgment or opinions. I fell into a deep state, this surge of energy overcame me!! I felt a deep connection to every living thing, as one, then the greatest love I ever felt, it took my breath away, the love of my true self, my soul. A love that did not feel like anything else. I've tried to find the best way to describe it, but no words truly describe what I had experienced. It's what's inside us all, pure light; it was the most beautiful, joyous feeling!! I wish I could find a way for all to feel their greatest love. If all could feel this once in their life, it could never be forgotten, and all would know what we are searching for. We would evolve quicker; we can have Heaven on Earth much sooner.

I finally found a part-time merchandising job. But unfortunately, I had fallen so far behind on my truck payment, so I had to turn it over. Fortunately, my sister and brother-in-law had an extra car, which I offered to pay for in February with my tax refund. I just needed to stay positive and determined. I tried to do what I could to keep the darkness from consuming me.

By the time December came along, my sister and brother-in-law offered us to stay with them (my mother was also living there to watch my niece during the day). My kids were happy to play with their cousin every day, having family around all the time and a backyard to play in. I offered to give them what I could toward utilities, but they wouldn't accept it. I would continue looking for steadier work &/or 2nd job here and there. My mom would watch the kids during the day, and I would do their lessons right after work. All was going smoothly, so I had no doubt I would have a place for us soon. Once I had alone time, which wasn't often, I spent it writing and re-reading my journal entries, returning to memories, trying to figure out what clues I had missed. Reflecting, reflecting, reflecting.

Journal: 01-03/2018

-Looking how much has passed, gone, just a memory, can't change the past...need a more steady, reliable job...not to give up...

-A higher connection to all...we could only ever go up, higher, brighter...self-knowledge is truly the greatest power...my energy feels different...how to find meaning in the real world...

-Need to focus...need to connect again...not enough me time...drained, unable to sleep, just want to rest...

-I've been sucked up into this game again...

Meditative writing:

"Practice quieting your mind, you will bring yourself to the message."

"Show how to love yourself."

-But why is my story important/different?

"Not different."

"We are all the same."

"How to find peace & happiness inside, forget all the noise around. Find a way to stay a step higher. All this will keep you down until you learn to always look pass it."

"To show how to find a way to create change."

-When will it change for me/us?...What am I missing?

-Not everyone will understand me. How can I help them understand?

-Why do I still feel shame around the ones closest to me?...Am I looking for acceptance? Do I still have undealt with issues to face with them?...Still feel low with them, but great at the same time...

-I have been practicing reminding self of who I am, can I always be without judgment?

-That's what all this has been about!!

"Just keep looking at the bigger picture."

"View how each soul are in their learning journey."

-Tired…hard to focus with the environment…too many interruptions…too many energies pulling my attention away…

-Frustration…fear of being stuck fills me…

-Tired of challenges…but there will always be challenges…I got this…

-Need to connect again…need to write, but can't focus…feel blocked…

One day an old low familiar feeling overcame me, but what was different was I recognized it.

-The moment of fear is where it starts…

I knew where it would drag me into a deeper, darker hole. I refused for it to overtake me; I pushed all those negative thoughts away. I felt free, in control, and in power for the first time. I felt my true self illuminating more from within and beginning to radiate out. For a moment, in my mind's eye, I could see and feel what it was like to make a deep connection with others; this would grow stronger in the years to follow.

-I can master overcoming fear…need to work more on it…

I had always done my taxes at the end of January to mid-February, and my refund in the bank not long after. When late March arrived, I was in for a surprise, *more* to try to understand and learn from–*and* still a long road before rest. Instead of a refund, I received a letter. The entire amount was applied to an old settled IRS account. My heart dropped; this was a mistake. This will delay everything, but I was confident it would be cleared away, and my refund would be sent out in two months at the latest. So, I returned to the tax woman who dealt with the IRS for me many years ago. She helped me so much I assumed she would take care of this quickly and easily. I had no worries; I figured I would hear something from her by the end of the week. Yet two weeks later, I still hadn't. I hesitated to call; I don't like to be pushy, and I need to be patient. At the end of the third week, and still not one word, I called. The receptionist wasn't the friendliest and was far from professional. When I asked to speak with the tax accountant, she turned me away, telling me she would contact me soon. Two more weeks passed, and not even an email, I called again, and the receptionist still wouldn't let me speak to her but told me they could only work with the IRS once I signed a form to allow them to. *I had been waiting this whole time, and nothing had been done!* I was so upset, yet I kept my composure and tried to stay positive. Then I received a letter from a collector about the truck I had repossessed. They had auctioned it off for about $1500 and billed me for $12,000!! I laughed to myself and tore it up. Even if I had the money, there was no way I would pay for a vehicle I didn't have; I didn't care how long it was to stay on my credit report. At this same time, I felt more and more uncomfortable at my sisters. I could sense an annoyance with us still being there. I was questioned more on how long it would be. I explained the situation on refund and gave them a time frame I *thought* would be. An agonizing month later, I finally got a call, not one I was hoping for. In short, my social security number was stolen and used to gain employment in California, which caused a domino effect on my past agreement with the IRS. So now this will take longer, which means more of a delay. I dreaded telling my sister. I know how they all see me, lazy, mentally unstable, and a leech. I had no idea what her reaction would be and what to do if she asked us to leave. Fortunately, she allowed us to stay with conditions, $400 a month, keeping her informed weekly where I'm at in apartment searching, and the kids needed to stay quiet downstairs in the early evenings.

I was constantly stressed, worried, and watching everything kids did, always on them to keep it down, stay out of the way, and not leave anything lying around. I felt I was robbing them of their childhood, all because I didn't want to upset anyone.

All those shadow energies, many times, found their way back into my mind as they became even harder to fight off. I hated living like this. I had many sleepless nights, crying and praying; I felt ashamed for not giving all my kids deserved. I went back and forth to put my kids in public school and work much more. But something inside would always whisper to me that it wouldn't make sense. I was different, these kids came to me for a reason. I needed to guide and teach them differently, I just needed to keep pushing through. "How can this world change if nothing is done differently?" I wanted, needed them to live in a completely different, better world. I needed to show them what it could be, and, more importantly, the tools for finding who they are and pushing out all the negative conditioning of this world. Even with what I knew, felt, and understood, I still had much more to learn. My stress never left me, but there were days I had layers of hope, energy, and faith. Meanwhile, I found a second part-time job in the evenings, which worked great. Between both, I was working seven days a week, about 10-20 daytime hours and 20 in the evenings. The best part of my job was that I could listen to music for nearly my entire shift. I consider it my only me time. I was able to perform my job very well, as my mind would also constantly think about my children, what I was able to do currently for them, what we could do together and working on resolutions. I would look at everything in my life, in the past and try to make sense of what I was to learn as well as what may be missing, just as I did before many years ago. My determination to get our place and imagining the smile and joy in my kids is what kept my strength up each day. By May, my first job hours changed slightly, ending in early evenings, overlapping with the second job. I needed to make a decision. Since the first job hours fluctuated, and mileage reimbursement doesn't change when gas prices increased; I benefit more from the second job. So, I put my notice in for the end of the month. Three days before that ended, I got unexpected news from my second job. I didn't know I wasn't making any more progress in training, so I was let go. I couldn't change my mind about my first job, as they had already found a replacement. So once again, I was about to be unemployed. I tried to look at everything positively, and everything happens for a reason. I felt I wasn't leaving with nothing, as I could see why I was at the second job for a short time; I needed to learn how to communicate better. To speak so much more clearly, with no stumbling, and able to find the right words to be understood as much as possible. Yet, I still struggled with the reality of my world; I had no income, no home, and dreamed of an unknown future.

Journal: 03-05/2018

-I had made a plan, A failed, B failed, C failed...I didn't have plan D...

-I'm a mother and need to care for my babies better...I need & want to be independent...

-I hate money, but need it...

-I don't want to live here anymore...

-Job searching like crazy...feel so stuck...clueless as to what's next...

-My babies deserve better...I deserve better...

-What do I know?...I have changed and grown, I fell behind in this world, I swear I only blinked...my world is standing still...

-Sleepless nights...scattered thinking...similar patterns...still need to let go of fear...

-Mind is sharper without mj...it has become an addiction...I've felt higher on my own...need to slow down...

-I try to meditate and pray silently to myself...Please help me find myself again, to energize my soul, feed my mind, to feel connected and be connected again...

-I just want...need to write...

-I want to be free...I want to move freely, probably why my knees make it difficult to...

At this point, I was determined to get anything, even if the hours were long, I just needed money and steady work hours. Fortunately, by the beginning of June, I was able to find a kitchen aid position. Daytime hours from 7am - 3:30pm, minimum wage, and it was nice to be off before sundown and weekends. Even though it was a very physical job and having the work of two people (a coworker out for medical reasons), I was just grateful to start saving again. They were flexible with me starting work a little later to drop kids off at school. It took some adjustments, just like anything new, but it eventually worked out smoothly. Sometime later, after work, my kids began telling me their grandmother would often try to convince them to attend public school, and kids would always tell her they were happy with their school. I didn't talk to my mother; I figured she would get it hearing it from kids. But day after day, kids would keep telling me they were tired of it. I finally mentioned it to my mother, who responded that kids are bored here all day. Even though I chose home school, it would only work if they were happy, if they wanted to see what public school was all about; I wouldn't deny them that, I'm always checking in with them. But they were, in fact, happy, they were not bored, they just wanted my mother to leave them alone about that. Even after I had spoken to her, she didn't. So now, this was weighing on my mind. She never supported my decision to homeschool and clearly didn't like having them during the day.

Not only was I working on myself but frustrated in trying to understand those close to me. Manipulative, controlling, judgmental, and just how I was spoken to as if I were unworthy. I understood their perspective on most things and why they believed what they did. But I couldn't come close to getting them to understand me and what I knew to be true. I had either lost them early on, or they had no interest in what I had to say and wouldn't get far, so they saw everything I did as wrong. But it still didn't make it okay to be how they were toward me, I just dealt with it as I always had. But when some of this behavior began being inflicted onto my children, I started seeing them very differently. I could see the confusion and hurt in my kid's eyes, I would find the best way to explain the reasoning behind their behavior, with the understanding that it's not them. So now I need to figure out who will watch my kids so I can switch to evenings. I needed to move quickly to get us out.

I then began recognizing how words didn't need to be expressed to know what others felt & thought. This is where I started to understand myself more and what I was capable of. I realized how I had done this many times in the past and was always right about what I was noticing. I started to pay more attention and put the pieces together to understand more of what I was completely feeling.

When August came, it was at this time I began noticing the similar abilities my son was coming into. The connection we shared and the way he would speak was way beyond lifetimes. This helped me see even more, I needed to stick to my path, do things my way, and find a way to make it work. Nearly every parent sees something special in their children. I have always felt a profound uniqueness in both of mine, my son is more sensitive and expressive, my daughter reserved and mysterious. Both brilliant and way beyond their years.

At this time, my sister announced she was expecting. We were all super excited and happy for them. But with this announcement came a time for us to be out–before the due date. I understood they were probably tired of helping, and we had already been there much longer than intended. It hurt, as they said they would need the space, even though they had plenty and we were staying in our mother's area, which was completely separate from theirs. I had no clue where we would go, I was just glad that our time here would be over, yet sad for the moments of joy we did have to be gone.

Journal: 09-10/2018

    -Still can't focus…drained…

    -No quiet or alone time…too many interruptions…chaotic environment…

    -I don't feel like doing this right now, if much at all, anymore…time is flying by…I can't focus, I'm tired…nothing I do changes…I'm tired of playing this game of survival…

    -Confusion, so lost, so alone, worthlessness, afraid of the endless cycle of struggle…I know it's all from fear, but I just can't seem to shake it…

    -I can't see any other logical way out…I hate that way, I'm tired of that way…it's not my way…but how else to survive and thrive?

    -I look back at my life from this point and wonder why I'm being held back & down…why can't I get ahead? How is what's calling me holding me back? What have I done? Is it just karma?

By November, with more complaints from my mother about my kids being homeschooled, I quietly put in my two weeks' notice. I didn't feel I had a choice, no daycare would take school-aged children, only after regular school hours. So, I called the same close friend (like father / grandfather), and without hesitation, offered us to stay with him as long as we needed; he even gave us his bedroom, with a twin bed for kids to share and a cot for me. Nearly every person in my life had judged me in some way, but he never had. I got up early, packed, cleaned up and left a thank you note. My mother was upset I left as I had, which I later realized I shouldn't have left as I did, but I just wanted to be gone. I didn't want to be in that energy anymore. I was tired of needing help but grateful for someone to have always been there. It took several nights of crying to release most of those low emotions and several days to feel much less stressed. My energy felt lighter, and I could think about what I needed to do to get back on track.

After a couple of weeks, I really needed complete alone time, as well as give my friend a break from us. I debated touching my savings but gave in and booked a four-night stay at a hotel for the kids and me. They were thrilled! The excitement and joy in their eyes when they saw two queen size beds, a huge screen tv with multiple options of what to watch, and all that space just for us three! They said it felt like a mini vacation. It was well worth it, it was a special moment for us, one we had needed for a long time. We stayed up late watching tv and cuddling, we slept in, the best sleep we all had in a very long time. It broke my heart knowing it would only be four nights, but grateful at least it was four.

I kept communication to the bare minimum with family, there was still quite a bit of tension. With holidays coming, I wanted it to be joyful, fun, and full of magic for kids, even though I would rather stay entirely away, we did get together for outings and gatherings.

I was finally able to get the kids' father to help by watching them in the evenings so I could work, with perfect timing to accept the first job offer. Thankfully not long after, I found a second job, temporary cleaning, a few hours past midnight and usually right after the first job. Management was kind and generous, as they had often left unsold food for me. Since getting off so late most nights, the kids would just stay over at their dad's new place, and I would get them in the mornings. We usually spend the day at the library to cover lessons and then head to the park. As it got colder, it was better not to take them out. I would go over to do their lessons and would leave as soon as we were done. I didn't feel comfortable being there at all, let alone when studies were done. That was the hardest, it hurt only seeing them for a few hours a day, not being able to tuck them in at bedtime and kiss them goodnight. But knowing they had a warm, safe space to play freely and feeling more comfortable than in any other place, brought me peace. I would still stay at my friend's some evenings & end up repeating the past, which is not worth repeating now. I would only sleep a few interrupted hours, get up early, sit at a fast food dine-in for hot coffee and breakfast, waiting to pick my babies up. I would listen to music, write, and reflect. Some days it wasn't all that bad, as I knew there was something to be gained from all this, and soon it would be in the past; it always passes.

Journal: 11/2018

-I don't know what direction to go...I feel trapped...doors unlocked, but dead end, eventually forced to turn around...

-Cloudiness...

-I could see the missing spaces of the puzzle: I just can't figure out what these pieces are...

-Why isn't God helping me? Why is it so hard for me to live simple? Why am I the way I am!? Why couldn't I just be!!??

-I HATE THIS PLACE!! I HATE IT SO MUCH!! WHY AM I HERE!!??

-I can't figure it out!! I'm tired...am I delusional?

-I thought being me and following this yearning would bring happiness, fulfillment...

-I feel like I'm running out of time...have I wasted my life?

-No work, no kids to look after or entertain right now, no place to be, sitting alone in car...need to try again, to focus...

-Let go of what I cannot control...

-Writing is soothing, words are clearer and understood...it's another way of coming out as I am, my true self, my way of connecting to self...

-I realized, with the first part of my journey, much still had been unknown, that path was exhausted, and it was time to come home, which meant to work when returning, but turned out so much more than imaginable, so if I do so now, take the only logical way out, what extraordinary thing will be awaiting?

-I need to go backward, remember where I was and where I am...how I started my journey, but how I was always filled with questions for as long as I can remember...I was meant to search and discover...I found my connection...I found a way, and I will find my own way...

-I need to help guide as many as possible...why is this important...the difference of knowing and feeling it all to connect together...we need to change, everything needs to change, or nothing will change...

-If I look from their perspective, how can I get them to understand?

Meditative writing:

"Stop trying to feel and see from them, it can be negative & judgmental, this doesn't matter."

"Focus on your perspective only, meditate, there's more, find it."

-God, please help me figure it out...

-I've had 35+ jobs, none of which made me happy, every one of them, I didn't feel I belonged...I don't know what else to do but the need to write...

Hope, faith, and clarity would return. It would go back and forth for years, as little by little, the light began illuminating more over the shadow, and I was able to overcome challenges with more ease.

A letter from the IRS had arrived, stating they were about to seize my bank accounts. I was so upset and panicking!! They are so quick to go after the little guys for whatever little bit they have!! I immediately drove to my tax accountant and once again dealt with their unprofessionalism, still trying to brush me away and making it difficult to return all my documents. Fortunately, another accountant stepped in, was willing to assist, and had everything ready to be picked up the next day. I needed to act quickly and found a real tax professional who was truly kind, honest, and helpful. On the same visit, he gave me two options; first, he was willing to help and deal with the IRS, and he explained what he would do, but it would cost quite a bit, or second, handle it myself, which he provided steps I could take. I've come across very few genuine people in my life who genuinely wanted to do what they could to help in those moments. What a difference it had made for me, how I've never forgotten, and how I held a place in my heart of prayer for them to be watched over and be given back what they had given me. I was so grateful for this gentleman's generosity and compassion. As soon as I returned to my car, I called the number he provided. I left a message and got a call back immediately. She removed the seized order and requested documents to be faxed. I couldn't believe it, I had been waiting all this time for this to be resolved, and now finally, it was moving along!

I began spending more time alone as most weekends were cold, and kids rather stay in at their dads playing. I was happy knowing they were happy and comfortable, but part of me was angry with not only myself but their father. If I had always had his help, I would have always been able to work; we wouldn't have ever been in this situation. Now he gets to have them, and my heart aches as I constantly pray for help getting a home. But I had enough frustration and stress, I didn't want anger to consume me, I needed to let it go and just be happy he was here now for our babies, and they were safe, warm, and comfortable. I needed to just put energy into what I did want and started thinking of what type of ideal work I would like that would fit us. So, I jotted it down in my journal and didn't put any more thought into it.

"An equal amount of sitting and on feet M-F, evenings, about 25 hours a week, ideal not to deal with customers and about $1500 a month…"

As Christmas came a week away, I was able to get a week's pay in advance to get my kids some gifts. I was so grateful, it seems nearly every Christmas, I am just able to make it for them. Their father also gladly allowed me to stay a few nights with them. We did spend Christmas with family, but again, I only did it for all the kids, fortunately it turned out to be peaceful and enjoyable.

Journal: 2019

    -I had a vivid dream last night, can't remember a whole lot, but I saw a woman (name starts with Z) whom I knew but never met in this life…she had light skin and long dark hair, leaning close to me beside the bed, she said…"Just keep coming back, you will figure it out"…after waking I thought about what she was talking about, I had been asking for help, felt alone and unheard, lost…I need to keep trying to reconnect...the feeling of someone really beside me reignited my fire, brought back hope, faith, and strength...

-Drained...but I can do this...

-Trying to find my way back...too much on my mind...

-I'm stuck, everything is too expensive, it's impossible to get out of this hole!

-How can I see anything better when for myself I am not moving!!

-What can I do for us 3? Not for anyone else anymore...when I think I can't get further down, I go deeper, deeper...further from the light...

-I'm ruining my babies' lives...who can help guide me in the way I need? Who would understand me? I can't help anyone if I can't help myself!!

-I tried to enjoy the simple things, but that's a struggle...without knowing what the future will bring, I can't relax!

-I'm tired...this has been going on way too long...why can't I manifest anything? What am I missing!?

-I just want to sleep...but keep waking to this nightmare over and over again...

-This can't be part of the plan...nothing makes sense...I just don't belong here...nothing has come to me besides my babies, which I'm also failing...

-I can't run...there's nowhere to go...no money...no direction...

-I don't belong...I don't belong...I shouldn't have been me...I destroyed my life...and my babies...

-Watching life pass me by...time wasted...don't want to be here...

-...but again...will try to connect...no energy though...

-Just write...write...write...it's quiet...my deep thoughts...I can almost...push all out...trying...the fears...the worries...the noise...it's so hard...feel the thoughts...they will just flow...finish my story...

-Trying again...concentrate...words...words...my words...I...feel...hurt...confusion...scattered...okay... trying again...same feelings as before about self...what is possible?...

-I can do this...focus...

Meditative writing:

"Church."

-A church??

"Children."

-Help children?

"Help show them the way."

-My children?

"It won't really show now. There is more."

"Everything isn't what can be seen but felt."

-I came into being lost…finding a way…

"Teach."

-I see! I see again!!

-I know happiness!! I know freedom!!

-They will remember! They will carry on!!

-It's more!! It's more than what we been wanting!! The greatest love!! It's in you!!!!!

-But more? I have a strong sense there is more…but I just can't figure it out…is there more? Is it too soon to know?

Every time I find that spark, I try with all my might to hang onto it, but this world makes it extremely hard as struggles to survive draw in the shadows over the light. I began practicing more by listening to what I'm feeling instead of what I think. I tried for the near future, fear echoing, saying the plans I had in mind wouldn't work. But when I pushed away that fear and felt what was hidden, peace and ease filled me, and knew all would be okay; it would get easier. Yet, I still struggled to release worries entirely and to trust.

Something that I needed to keep working on.

    -Still need to understand where to stand, what I know to be true, and what is...

    -Still feel like I have absolutely no control...

    -I tend to leap before looking...may not always be good...but maybe it's just faith...

    -I had always felt empty till my babies came to me, then I found myself...

    -I've tried to find my place in this world, but it doesn't fit me...so I will create my own...

    -I know who I am, it's never been more clearer...I need to learn to keep standing firmly and see that the darkness is just trickery...the direction to myself is all that makes sense...to go against it is what feels wrong...I didn't waste time...I've been working hard to find me...

I would fall into a deep battle with myself. Mixed emotions, uncertainty, and negativity. Even with some positiveness, such as the kid's father kindly letting me stay more evenings to be with kids, encouraging dreams, I *knew* were messages and slowly having family around. But the reality of everything, still in the same place, held me down. I struggled each day to get through acceptance and understanding. My frustration and impatience spilled at times onto my babies. I started forcing myself away to avoid being like that toward them. I tried to seek help from public housing but was turned away. I researched to see what I needed to do to buy a home in the future or even just a small loan to put towards an apartment, that is, once I'd be earning more, but it all turned out to be nearly impossible. I looked into repairing credit, but the process would cost money I didn't have, and for something I could do on my own, with effort and time. I didn't know what to do anymore or whom to turn to. I couldn't let this entire system keep me down, there's a reason for all this never to have worked for me. Besides not caring to understand it all, if I had played it right, that would mean I would have perceived things differently and lived a different life, I wouldn't be who I am. So, this is another thing I needed to figure out in my own way. I need to make a solid plan. I really need to balance my spiritual life with physical. I need to keep focus, I was determined to find a job that would fit us, so I could continue homeschooling & writing. I just hope their father will keep helping by watching them in the evenings.

By March, I was depleted trying to balance our routine. Kids and I would still go back and forth from their fathers, my friends, the storage unit, hours at library & park (when there was nowhere else to go) and work. I had now been dealing with constant pelvic pain that was progressing and requiring all sorts of tests. I was confident it would be a quick, easy fix. With so much to already juggle, this made it more challenging. It felt like one step forward, two steps back. I would pray for more strength and grasp harder onto my faith. As my darkness kept looming, I realized what was on replay in my mind was holding me down, draining me, and not allowing me to enjoy life. I had no control at this moment for what was, but I did have control of changing my mindset. I tried harder to enjoy each day more, alone and with my kids. Even with little to no money, I would think of simple things to do. I would tuck my emotions away and try to keep all stress and frustration at bay. I needed my kids, as well as myself, not only to know but to believe we would be okay and to remember what was important, that we have each other, we are healthy, to always be grateful for what we do have, and always make the best of it. This wasn't my plan in raising children, but it must have been part of a plan. They've come to understand, in their experience, what other children go through, and it has opened their hearts to more compassion toward others. Eventually, they will see there is no perfection, no mistakes, just lessons and a reason for everything.

By April, we had welcomed a new addition to the family, my beautiful, healthy nephew. Such an incredible blessing to have more children in our family, it makes life so much more hopeful & joyous and another reason to keep pushing forward.

Then finally, the IRS sent me a check for a portion owed. A huge relief, yet fear still had its grasp, and I didn't feel it was enough to put toward an apartment. So, I decided to wait and continued as we were. I began looking into everything around me for more meaning.

Each interview I had, I looked beyond why I was there, what I was to learn in those moments and practice to what I was sensing if the job was going to or not be given to me, and what the general feel of the environment was. I began recognizing a familiar feeling of a surge of energy. A sense of fresh air, a change, something new and good coming. I had yet to understand these surges, as I've never really paid much attention to them in the past, but I began taking note of them, as many, many more would come to be understood.

As the year progressed, it did become much smoother, easier, and more enjoyable, with more ups than downs. While job searching, I came across a position I'd never expected. At a donation warehouse, permanent evenings, 3:30-8:30 pm, M-F, perfect pay. I went to the interview and found out exactly what the job entailed. No customers, scanning books (which I absolutely love books!) & media, checking quality and list online, I would have equal sit and on feet and be allowed to have headphones on!! Even benefits for part-time!! I was hired on the spot!! I was so thrilled, happy, grateful, and in disbelief!! I prayed and thanked God!! I knew this was the beginning of a new phase, finally the change I'd been waiting for!!

Even though we were spending more joyous time together with family, I still found my mind at full speed when around them and always paying attention to what energy I was sensing. I always knew what was about to steam but didn't always listen to those feelings. It took many falls into the deep darkness from their inflictions to take a stance for my self-worth and put distance throughout the year. As December rolled in, I was preparing for an outpatient surgical procedure. Gratefully my family helped care for my children and me as I was healing. From what I discovered and came to believe; we have the ability to heal ourselves. Our minds are so much more powerful than we realize, we need to understand what the body is trying to tell us, and heal the mental &/or emotional connection, which I tried myself, but maybe I still needed more to learn, &/or it must have carried on too long, becoming more difficult to heal this way. Even though this was a very safe procedure, fear did creep into my mind, wondering how my children would be if I were to pass, if how I had been raising them was worth it. I then fought that thought, I reminded myself that fear was trying to control me again and that I knew better. I put my focus back into my intuition, knowing I would be okay and looking forward to the relief of pain. This was also the opportunity to slow down and look more into what else I needed to heal from before it started affecting my physical health again.

By January 2020, I just wanted to be. Near the end of the month, I finally got the rest of what the IRS owed me; with a stable income, I decided to pay weekly at a hotel in the safer part of the city. It would be our temporary home for the next six months, meanwhile searching for an affordable apartment. Having a real bed to sleep in was the best feeling for us. The best rest we had in a long time. We felt joy, comfort, and safety being together every night and knowing it was our space.

As the cold weather approached, our car began breaking down. Instead of getting a newer used car before the problem progressed, the fear of being unable to afford the payments stopped me, so I decided to keep shopping around. I ended up spending hours back and forth at multiple dealerships, most cars were older, had over 100,000 miles & cost way more than they should. When I found a great deal, I couldn't get anywhere, as the finance guy was never in the office (later, I would find out these cars were marked as a total loss). We had to deal with pulling over every so many miles on each trip we made, in below freezing temperatures for two weeks and taking us hours to get to the hotel after work. We ended up making a trip to the ER because the cold triggered my daughter's asthma, all because of my fear. That weekend I returned to the very first dealership offer, and once the financing process started rolling, it turned out my monthly payments would be much less than what was estimated. This process went smoother than any other time. Plus, the car was only five years old with only about 40,000 miles, excellent gas mileage, and interior purple neon lights, my favorite color! It felt like I was being told to let go, trust, the change is here, we got you. To have the funds to put towards a down payment on this car & afford a safe place for us during the lockdown, the timing couldn't have been more perfect. I needed to trust more and let go of control.

For the next six months, the kids and I spent time watching movies and playing together, going out to the park (empty parking lots for a while) more freely, knowing we could return to our temporary home whenever we wanted. We talked about what we would want in a future home. From how we could imagine our house, the pets we wanted, and what we could do in our permanent place. Even if we couldn't have a big house right away, we would be grateful and happy to have a small cozy apartment, it would still be home. We prayed all the time in gratitude for what we did have, for our continued health and safety, and for that of the world. I truly began letting go and trusting more. I tried, even more, to live in the moment, well making my way into learning to balance everything out. I continue putting my children and myself ahead from letting any low energies come around. As soon as I felt some family were back at making comments, being judgmental, or just thinking what they're saying is positive in trying to convince me to be someone I wasn't, I reverted to going back to staying away, more so during this time, cutting back on communications. I recognized what a difference it made in my energy. At times it would seep through into me, this is when I began learning how to really push it out more, away, and close that door to the darkness.

I began having more & more vivid dreams, some about my near and far future, the physical & spiritual realities. Then about the world's future, which I didn't understand at the time, but I would journal and study them. It wouldn't be until it happened that I understood, so when I had more of the same, I knew what it meant and what was coming.

Journal: 02-06/2020

 -Symbolic of that of the world...a female voice saying,

 "Only if we come together or no future..."

 -A dream and another, which was quite long, but in short, I felt the fear, pushed the fear aside, and walked through that door...a knowing came to me that I was safe, we were safe...fear is an illusion...I was in control...I transformed the darkness into light...

 -Several dreams most into the far future...coming out to show who I am and what I was able to do...healing the world through pure energy...a master in that ability...to be free...

 -I need to understand my energy more... With more dreams, I felt I was being shown my doubtful mind what my yearnings were leaning towards. The searching and questioning returned, along with the excitement of what else I would possibly discover about myself. Flashes of random, long, forgotten memories and the emotions I felt in those moments would come and go. It felt like I was being reminded my journey had started since I had come into this world, that every moment of life was important, and it was building up to the moment of awakening. We come into this world with love, that in itself always feels like home. I began feeling more lost and confused when love was nearly completely gone for me around nine. When it reignited in my early 20's, I felt closer to home.

With what was happening worldwide, it was easy to see why. As long as I can remember, I have always felt I was anticipating for a key moment to come into the world to indicate a significant change coming. A plan for something greater. We can no longer continue as we are; we're barely evolving, the anger, fear, and violence keeps repeating. So, when the pandemic came, I knew that was the sign; it was time for a major shift in consciousness. But I wanted to know for sure what it all really meant, so I decided to ask my Angels and Guides, hoping, but not expecting anything. "Why is this all happening? What does this really mean?" Less than an hour later, just before getting to work they told me in the same way as they do when I'm in deep meditation.

"It's an energy shift."

-It makes sense!! Why didn't I think of that!! That's why it affects everyone differently!!"

Even with this understanding, my heart ached for the pain the world was feeling with so many souls leaving. I'm sure nearly everyone suffered the loss of a loved one this year, one way or another.

In June, our family lost my beloved uncle. I love my Tio so much. It'd been such a long time since I had seen him. Remembering him when he was much younger as a strong handyman, and the love and knowledge he had for cars, he would always be willing to help and give what he could. I had the chance to see him in February, but "*FEAR*" of taking more time off filled me; I had just returned to work after some time off for recovery from surgery. I usually would just have gone, not caring about work, but I was trying to do things differently to get us a home. I thought I had more time. I imagine the reunion he must have had with his parents, how much they had loved each other in life. I would later dream of him being healthy, strong, happy, and free.

At the end of August, we drove to California for his memorial service. It was wonderful to see family again after so many years; I wished it were under different circumstances. The deep aching and silence that echoed in their hearts was unbearable. There were things I had recognized long ago about myself and the abilities that lie within, but still left me confused because I had no control. I would randomly hear familiar and unfamiliar voices. One late night working alone in a small cafe cleaning, I heard a very familiar sound. My grandfather, who passed many years before, would always loudly clear his throat; I instantly recognized it; I knew he was visiting me. During my uncle's memorial dinner, which had taken place in an average sized pizzeria packed with about 200 family and friends, multiple conversations carrying on over loudly playing music, just barely able to hear the person sitting right next to me, I heard a clear, loud male voice call out my name and something else in Spanish. It was like a loud clap to get my attention; I looked around to see who it could be, but it came from an area where no one was, and it was so clear over all the noise. I do not speak or understand much Spanish, so I had no idea what was said, but I knew it was my uncle. I wanted to share this experience, but I didn't feel it was time to mention anything. I stayed more alert, hoping to hear something or notice more signs.

When July arrived, I had yet to find an affordable place; I would have to work multiple jobs to make 3x the rent. Even before the pandemic, I've got to mention that other families were already living in the hotel. The cost of housing keeps rising; there's no excuse; it's just pure greed; it always starts from point A, then creates a domino effect. It was time for me to consider doing things differently because I could no longer afford a hotel. The kids returned to stay with their father, and I was alone again. I decided to find a second job for late evenings and save as much as possible. I needed to get out of this cycle.

In mid-September, I started working about 12 hours a week in a janitorial position. I enjoyed working alone, just deep in my mind. I've worked janitorial for a total of about eight years in my life, and it's physically exhausting. Cleaning should be one of the highest paying jobs, and just like everyone should work fast food and retail, everyone should work janitorial; people would be more considerate.

By October, the relationship with family had gotten even smoother. My mother would often have kids and me overnight on weekends. Not only was I grateful to be with my kids every weekend, but I enjoyed spending time with her, as we shared common interests. Maybe I also projected a different energy, and it was known we could leave whenever we wanted; we had other options, there was no control, and I would stand firmly for who I was. One late evening (kids and I were sleeping on the living room floor, myself in the middle), I had awoken suddenly and turned around to go back to sleep, but I didn't get to that sleep state, but in-between. I was alert, awake, but couldn't move; I heard a male voice, whispering, as not to wake anyone, speaking to someone else; they were just a couple of feet near my daughter. My natural mother's reaction was panic, but I couldn't move or turn to see who it was. I couldn't make out anything but one word, motel & I knew they were talking about us; I was trying to keep my mind calm as my heart was racing. They must have known I was aware; in that state, as I was trying to come out of it, I felt his presence lean in closer; my mind panicked more as I knew he was closer to my daughter, but as he leaned in he was saying "Shh" & kissed me on my forehead and I instantly came out of it. I opened my eyes as my heart pounded, but I had no fear & knew something incredible had just happened; I didn't even move or look around; I closed my eyes, hoping I could return to that state, but didn't. How and why did this happen? Was it because I'm always envisioning my Angels, Guides beside me? Because I often talk to them? Had I always been trying to connect that the veil has become thinner? Or because I had been asking for more signs? I was in awe and disbelief; this amazing experience solidified what I've always felt to be true; there is so much greater going on beyond our world.

Towards the end of October, I had enough saved that it was time for apartment hunting again. I hoped to find anything, even if it were just a studio, but I was prepared to make multiple contacts, negotiate, and accept what would be.

But everything just seemed to fall into place with little effort. The first listing I found accepted previous evictions with a double deposit coming to only $500, way less than I anticipated, leaving me with savings to stay ahead. It was an affordable one-bedroom apartment, a much older complex, but in an okay neighborhood. I was the first to apply, and we moved in the first week of November. The joy, excitement, and relief in knowing we had a safe, permanent home and just in time for the holidays, we were beyond grateful!! All I wanted now was to experience our way of a normal life in a home raising my children. With no worries about where we will be next week or month, what we can or can't do, or having to go to storage to pick out the next seasonal outfits. We finally could enjoy the things we had talked about together. To be cozy in our home when it was cold out. I spent so much time fighting not to follow the general way; I was afraid I would lose myself if I worked and lived like society. But I see it clearer now. To have faith and trust in a higher power is to relinquish control. I had in the past little bits here and there, but I hadn't realized I was holding on too tight and not releasing enough. Everything just seemed so surreal to finally have the changes I had needed, hoped, and prayed for.

Mid-January, we were well into our routine, which I enjoyed, especially the daily tasks for kids I couldn't do before. But I began noticing what I didn't want; to feel entrapped and consumed by work. I know I need to play the game and work to pay for the things to help us live more comfortably, but having just two days off a week isn't enough. It makes sense why the world is lost; who has time to search for more? I've fallen into that wheel. I had done it in the past and didn't understand how to make adjustments to make it work. So, I needed to figure out how to balance it out my way.

Journal: 01-02/21

-More dreams of flying…freedom…

-Thinking of leaving 2nd job…but back and forth, that additional money helps…fear looming again, will I make the wrong decision and screw up…I could take a couple of months off to clear my mind & write…to connect…

-This emptiness is still echoing…weekends come and go; I don't seem to have time for self…

-Tired again to meditate early in morning…

Meditate writing:

"…Keep going…"

-Tried again but then found myself falling asleep while fighting it, then came to an in-between state, heard a male voice call out my name…tried to focus, but came fully awake...

    -Going over the same questions, looking for a different answer...

    -Vivid dream...flying, reaching out my hand behind me, envisioning my Angels holding my hand...then suddenly I saw and felt a hand reach into mine, an Angel appeared...this Angel appeared as male. Three female Angels were flying behind him, another male behind them, and I felt two more behind him. When we landed, I could see most of their faces...the first male had light skin and hair (his energy felt like the male that I heard when I was in the inbetween state months ago), 2 of the females were just a bit darker with cornrows, and the other female had light skin, the other male wasn't clear he stood a bit back and the other two still not visible...I had awoken still feeling each with me as I now felt they had answered my question about how many were with me...

    -So, I decided to give a month's notice for 2nd job...I will spend more time on myself...if need be, I can always return to this job...

Over the next couple of months, management at the apartment complex was constantly changing, and nothing was getting anywhere with a leaking ceiling, broken fridge & now roaches. As much of an annoyance and frustrating as it was, I understood what was happening. I was being tested to see what I would do, if I would walk away. I was not going to repeat any part of the past. After more attempts in trying to reach out to someone, I decided to research renters' rights, then passed on that information to the highest management and immediately got a response; within days everything was taken care of.

Throughout the year, drama from a co-worker would try to get me involved or target just me in his nonsense. Most times, I simply kept to myself and ignored everything, but other times I found myself fighting his low energies. I was able to master doing my job, while studying the energy around me. This is when I really began learning more about energy and my abilities. It was like a light switch, which was always on. Instantly all at once, I would get a rush of someone's energy, telling me their deepest shadow emotions and to possibility why those came to be. I soon came to realize why I couldn't handle being around crowds. The energies of others would spill onto me, which was confusing, overwhelming, and exhausting. When it was anger, I felt their fear and needed to stay away; when it was sorrow, I could feel their pain, as they felt it, which was way too much. So now I was learning how to decipher my energy from others, and with this co-worker's constant low vibrations. I found my off switch. I began repeating to myself, "It's not my energy, it's not my energy, it's not my energy, I'm okay, everything is okay," then envisioned a white light barrier surrounding me. It worked. I used it everywhere I went, especially before leaving home. In June, I struggled to get much writing or anything in self-growth done. Frustrated with the lack of energy and the feeling of not getting anything more accomplished, but then realized it's not time for movement, but rest and rejuvenation. Years of constantly searching, moving, and sleepless nights, no wonder why I'm so tired. I don't need to worry; we're good; it's okay to rest and take it easy.

The entire year was filled with much comfort and blessings. Relationship with the kids' father had become stronger with more support and closer friendship. With family, there was more respect for boundaries and most times getting along rather well. We lived more comfortably than ever. Work was still going great, adding to my savings, and finances kept flowing to us from different avenues. I was able to comfortably buy my kids not only what they needed but what they wanted. We enjoyed many outings, and the best part was taking a first family 11-day vacation, easily with no financial worries. Finally in October, my kids & I adopted two furry members into the family.

I had realized how this all came to be. I had put in mind what I wanted, the ideal type of work, and how we would like to comfortably live and then let it go. My grandpa tried to explain to me, way before I could understand that everything is energy. So just putting a thought into something takes energy; you're sending an energetic vibration into the universe of what to attract to you. So even thinking what you don't want is still sending that signal. Changing my perspective of money changed my energy towards it. I no longer thought of money as negative, just neutral. I stopped thinking about the lack of it. I no longer worried about how much was in my bank account. I would manage what was there responsibly, but also, at times, send a quick thought to what I envision to be in there. Having the material things money can buy to make life more comfortable and enjoyable is nice but having each other is everything. Gratitude is one of the greatest vibrations; we are always giving our thanks with every prayer. We still have lessons to grow from, and some things we ask for won't come to us right away, or maybe not at all. We will be turned around or blocked if it's not the best for our personal growth.

I've learned I'm being guided and need to trust where I'm being led; there's a balance of control in working with my Guides, Angels, God, and the Universe. Also, acknowledging the signs given, I had so many about the same thing; yet my doubtful mind would question it over and over again. When it was really important, they would make it undeniable. For example, nearly 2 years ago, a gentleman stopped just a few feet in front of me, on the back of his jacket in huge print read, "Share Your Story." Another thing I came to understand was, some of these jobs I had would have pushed me out eventually. I would later learn about ownership changes, layoffs and others completely shutting down. I wasn't meant to put much energy into a job; the energy was supposed to go into discovering more of myself. When enough was gained, and it was time to put it together, the availability and comfort came to be. I was always searching for more, focusing on what was beyond. I struggled to understand this world and how to live in it, eventually learning and balancing both. Recognizing most times how my physical world mirrored what was going on inside, bringing to light what I needed to work on.

I've learned to make sense of my past; life isn't meant to be easy; things just don't happen; we just need to look at the shadows from a different angle.

I've learned to do my best to keep all forms of negative vibrations energies away, including choosing what I watch, limited social media and news. As well as listening to mostly high-vibrating, inspiring, empowering music, filled with love, kindness, and hope. Their powerful words and melody vibrated so strongly, especially when helping me out of my darkness, which reignited my light. Also, what I put in my body, more whole foods, fresh produce, which in itself carries high vibrations. And finally, completely cutting out low vibrational mind-altering substances, such as alcohol and marijuana.

I've learned I'm free to be me, stop looking for acceptance, let go of the fear of judgment, comparison, and release all negative beliefs of self that echo from others. I know it was my own determination, faith, and unwillingness to give up, but I didn't find my way on my own. Not only were my Angels and Guides helping me along, but also the many people I've come across. The genuine kindness in simple gestures or conversations vibrated hope for humanity and an instant soul connection of love.

I do believe we can still grow without the darkness, anger, fear and violence. It's time to leave all this in the past and really learn from history instead of repeating it. I fought long and hard to find my way through the unknown. I held onto my faith, prayed, leaped, and stood strong and firmly in what I felt and believed so deeply inside. I came to understand the clues and found the pieces of my jigsaw. I made sense of my darkness by illuminating, understanding, and healing it forever. I found my way to peace, happiness, and my greatest love. Once you feel the love of self, loving every living thing is easy. I'm here to help spread positive energy, help create change, and to save our world.

This is my truth, my words, my voice, my story.

www.ingramcontent.com/pod-product-compliance
Lightning Source LLC
Chambersburg PA
CBHW032125090426
42743CB00007B/472